CALLING GIPPSLAND HOME

Famous Men and Women of Gippsland

More Books by Jim Connelly

Tom and Anna on the Trail: the Case of the Missing Schoolgirl (2014)

Tom and Anna in Danger: the Case of the Disappearing Dogs (2014)

Tom and Anna take a Chance: the Case of the Bungling Bird Bandits (2015)

My Folk: Four Hundred Years of Hazards, Tooths, and Connellys (2015)

Mountain Boy (2016)

Talk of the Town: Warragul/Drouin (2017)

Talk of the Town: Warragul/Drouin (2) (2018)

Pickled Pieces and Rollicking Rhymes (2019)

Wild Beauty (2019)

Round and About in Gippsland (2020)

Father Jeremy (2020)

Growing up in Garfield (2021)

Stories of old Gippsland (2022)

CALLING GIPPSLAND HOME

Jim Connelly

Copyright

Copyright Jim Connelly 2023

Paperback ISBN 978-0-6486658-5-4

All rights reserved

No part of this publication may be reproduced or transmitted in any form or by any means, electronic or mechanical, including photocopying, recording, or any information storage or retrieval system, without prior permission of the copyright owner.

A CIP catalogue record for this book is available from the National Library of Australia.

First published in Australia 2023 by

James Timothy Connelly

12 Craig Street,

Warragul, Victoria, 3820

AUSTRALIA

ajcon@dcsi.net.au

For Stephen, Rodney, Meredith, Lyndel, Jennifer, and Alan

Cover design by Craig Braithwaite, *aussiepics*

The image on the cover of this book contains an image used under creative commons licensing.
Attribution; "Description: "Prostanthera galbraithiae" (cultivated, labelled), Royal Botanic Gardens, Melbourne, Australia |Source: digital photograph by author |Date:2009-09-16 |Author: Melburnian"

Please refer to Chapter 7: Jean Galbraith

CONTENTS

Mary Grant Bruce	9
Sir Frank Macfarlane Burnet	23
Helen Caldicott	37
Grace Jennings Carmichael	51
Geoffrey Cornish	67
Ada Crossley	82
Jean Galbraith	96
Sir Keith Hancock	111
Bertha McNamara	125
Lionel Rose	137
Sir Stanley Savige	150
David Williamson	165

CALLING GIPPSLAND HOME

Foreword

Someone once said to me that they believed Gippslanders suffered from an inferiority complex. Sealed off from the rest of Australia by the mountains and the sea, they felt aggrieved, that no-one else understood them, that others looked down on them. Maybe there's something in it. If there is still a lingering feeling of self-doubt, let this book be a comfort and corrective. Here are twelve eminent Australians who have lived part of their lives amongst us and about whom we might truly say that they called Gippsland home.

Some lived in the east, some in the west; some came from South Gippsland and some from the Valley. Six are women, six men. All but one were born in Australia. The 'oldest' was born in 1853, the 'youngest' in 1942. Two are still living. Twelve different occupations are covered by these twelve people. They are arranged here in alphabetical order.

Choosing twelve meant not choosing many more. My original list numbered twenty-one and others were quickly added by those who knew of my undertaking. Perhaps there is another book to be written and perhaps another person to write it. Certainly Gippsland abounds in men and women who have become or are becoming leaders in their field. All cannot but be touched by the gentle graciousness that lies at the heart of this Gippsland of ours.

Jim Connelly, August, 2023

MARY GRANT BRUCE

... a Gippslander with roots going back to the earliest years of settlement, who immortalised Gippsland bush life in her children's novels, who travelled far from home but loved to come back to these green pastures.

She was born Minnie Grant Bruce, but her publisher thought Mary Grant Bruce had a better ring to it, so that's what she became. Her family goes back to the Gippsland of the 1830s. William Whittakers, her grandfather, held the Snowy River run in 1839 and later moved on to 'Tombong', then 'Tubbutt', then down to the plains, to 'Loy Yang'. He finished up at 'Fernhill', outside Traralgon. There's a Whittakers Road there to remember him and the family by. Mary spent a lot of time on her grandfather's places when she was growing up. When she later wrote about galloping horses, she knew what she was talking about! Mary was greatly influenced by a feisty beloved aunt, 'Aunt Martha', who lived with Mary's family for many years.

Mary's mother, Minnie Whittakers, herself had a bush pedigree, having been brought up on the Monaro. Minnie married Lewis Bruce, a surveyor, originally from Cork in Ireland. His brother was the Very Reverend Charles Saul Bruce, a notable Dean of Cork. Lewis Bruce worked on many projects in Gippsland, including the

Black-Allan line, the boundary between Victoria and New South Wales. We might think of Lewis Bruce every time we visit the Sale racecourse, for it was he who laid it out. Our Mary Grant Bruce was born in 1878, the fourth of five surviving children. One of her brothers, sadly, was accidentally shot and killed by a playmate when aged eight – a tragedy that was to eerily reappear in Mary's life.

Her surveyor-father settled the family in a home, 'Mia Mia', on the edge of Sale, on the Maffra Road. After learning her lessons at home until the age of ten, Mary went to Miss Estelle Beausire's Ladies College in Stawell Street, later Cunninghame Street, the first secondary school for girls in Gippsland. The school, though it never had more than forty pupils, undertook 'thorough work in every branch of education – English, French, Latin, and Music'. Mary was a star pupil, matriculating with honours in English, History and Botany. She had been writing stories from the age of seven. In her teens she won the Melbourne Shakespeare Society's essay prize three years in a row. Mary wasn't one to hide her light under a bushel. She continued to enter literary competitions into her 'twenties.

In 1898, aged twenty, Mary set off, 'with five pounds in her pocket', to try her luck in the city. She boarded for a while with her old headmistress, now in Melbourne, Mademoiselle Beausire, and then moved out to live in a 'bachelor flat'. Mary was a spirited young woman. She bought herself a three-speed bike to get around town, and occasionally rode it home to Traralgon! This was at the time when women wore skirts down to the ankle! Her first job was as a secretary, but she had become known to the editor of the *Leader*, a weekend supplement to the *Age*, through her stories. Consequently, Mary was appointed editor of their children's page, continuing, however, to send stories and articles to a great range of journals and magazines. She was determined to make a name for herself.

Mary wrote a series of stories about children in the bush for the *Leader*. Later, they were put together and published under the title, *A Little Bush Maid*. It was Mary's first published work, and remains the best seller of all the multitude of books that followed. *A Little Bush Maid* has all the ingredients that made Mary Grant Bruce's books so popular. The opening lines immediately convey the essence of the Billabong books:

Norah's home was on a big station in the north of Victoria – so large that you could almost, in her own phrase, "ride all day and never see anyone you didn't want to see", which was a great advantage in Norah's eyes. Not that Billabong Station ever seemed to the little girl a place that you needed to praise in any way. It occupied so very plain a position as the loveliest part of the world!

As for the whole sweep of the book, perhaps we can let the publisher's blurb give its flavour:

A Little Bush Maid is the story of 12-year old Norah Linton. She lives at 'Billabong', her family's large and prosperous cattle station in country Victoria in the early 1900s. Norah has her very own pony, Bobs. She likes nothing better than riding Bobs and helping muster the cattle. Norah's widowed father and the station hands dote alike upon her. But for all their attention, she's a bit of a tom-boy.

Norah's brother, Jim, is home on holiday from boarding school with his friend Wally, and there is always plenty happening. Adventures and surprises abound at 'Billabong'. Contending with thieving swagmen, a maliciously-lit grass fire and riding accidents make for a full summer.

The circus comes to the district town, Cunjee. A fishing trip to a nearby creek results in unexpected drama when the children discover a mysterious stranger camped in the bush. Who is this hermit and why is he there? The man seems friendly, but later Norah learns that the Police are out looking for the Winfield Murderer. Mr Linton has gone to Sydney about some cattle. Norah's resourcefulness is tested to the full!

There followed the famous Billabong series of books – fifteen in all, the last being published in 1942 when Mary was sixty-four. The best known, probably, were *Jim and Wally, Back to Billabong, Billabong's Daughter*, and *Billabong's Luck*, though I expect many Billabong lovers to disagree with that selection. Jim and Norah are the hero and heroine. Wally is Jim's good friend. The Linton family is heavily idealised. To today's ear the stories may appear cloying, even saccharine, but they were written a hundred and more years ago when 'children were children', ready to be thrilled by tales of romance and adventure. Part of the charm of the Billabong books comes from the illustrations. Most of these were the work of a British artist – simply known as 'J. MacFarlane' – who captured the spirit of Grant Bruce's books in his flowing lines and striking sense of composition.

The Billabong books – and indeed the other Grant Bruce children's books as well - run around a handful of bush themes. They're set in a squatter's world. The children go to board at expensive city schools. They bring friends home for the holidays. There is tension between the bushwise Linton children and the sometimes rash city visitors. The books are redolent with the atmosphere of the bush – cattle mustering and branding, camping out, Chinese cooks, snakes, kangaroos, goannas and all the picturesque features of high-country Gippsland bush life. The wide open spaces and the luminous beauty of the Australian landscape are the background to every turn of the story.

And then there are the dangers and difficulties - bushfire above all, but there are also wild cattle and falls from galloping horses. Drought is a constant menace. Forest re-growth and bracken are invading the pasture land. There are cattle rustlers and suspicious characters lurking in the forest. If the book is set in wartime, there are potential enemy agents to be found. Above all, there is action, a new adventure, every day.

Grant Bruce's vintage years were from just before the First World War, through the 'twenties and into the early 'forties. These were the years that Australian national pride was at its height. The nation was very Anglo-Saxon; its eyes were fixed firmly on the wide open spaces of the countryside; it was a country building towards a glorious future. The Billabong series drew on these views and prejudices and helped to fix them firmly in the national psyche. Hard work was to be rewarded. Heroism and self-sacrifice were placed high on the spectrum of moral values. Mateship and the digger spirit of the First World War were promoted as a way of life. Women were to be homemakers, cheerfully submitting to the hardships of the day in order to serve the greater good. Hospitality was a key virtue. The children of her fiction were object-heroes for all Australian youngsters – from both city and country - to follow. She promoted a belief in the future greatness of our country. Loyalty and comradeship were values to be promoted and rewarded. Her leading characters are always earnest, purposeful, generous in spirit, and spotlessly clean in 'thought, word and deed'. Bruce is holding up an ideal for young people to follow, yet never pointing out the moral, but letting the actions speak for themselves. A writer in the *Weekly Times* in 1927 summed up the moral intention behind the stories as follows:

Consciously or unconsciously, there is high purpose in Mary Grant Bruce's writing. It leads, cleverly beguiling the way through tangled bushland, to an ideal of conduct insensibly presented to the eyes of her young readers. The fun and the frolic; the laughter and the tears; the exuberant spirits and the daring mischief — these are but vehicles gaily painted, garlanded with flowers as they may be, for teachings fundamentally essential to youth who would, in maturity, greatly attempt and greatly achieve.

Despite the lesser role given to the place of women in her books, Grant Bruce saw herself as standing up for women in a man's world. In her earlier career she combined with other women to form the Writers' Club in Melbourne, which later merged with the Lyceum Club. During the Second World War she worked for the AIF Women's Association. She wrote enthusiastically about the work of the women deaconesses in the Diocese of Gippsland who were doing heroic work, especially in the difficult forest country to the north. The citation for her induction into the Australian Media Hall of Fame reads:

At one stage she travelled around South Australia with political activist Muriel Farr on a tour for the Australian Women's National League to encourage women to vote. Later she was editor of the League's magazine, 'Woman'.

Grant Bruce wrote forcefully about women's issues. Women should have access to proper sex education. They should be able to take on a wider range of careers, if they wanted. Wives should have a defined allowance from their husbands to allow them independence.

Though remaining Australian to the core, Mary Grant Bruce became a citizen of two worlds – the old and the new. In 1913 she went to London where she wrote for the *Daily Mail*. The next year she met a distant cousin, Major George Bruce, from Co. Cork in Ireland, a retired British army officer. They had more than a common name: George was also a writer of fiction as well as learned articles on marine life. The two became engaged and came back to Melbourne to be married at Holy Trinity Church in East Melbourne. The First World War broke out just at this juncture and George was called up for military duties. They returned immediately to Britain, where George spent the war as a training officer in Ireland. Although the storm clouds of rebellion and civil war were gathering in Ireland, Grant Bruce played down the troubles there:

I worked in seven different places during the war - six in England and one in Ireland - and in no place was there such wonderful organisation and such concentrated war work as in Cork. Quite 95 per cent of the Irish people are loyal to Britain. The other 5 per cent are swayed by a few hot-headed fools. There was no sectarian bitterness in Ireland during the war. All religions and all grades of society worked hand in hand.

Mary was engaged in charity work on behalf of the war effort, while two sons, Jonathan (Jon) and Patrick, were born during the war years – and Mary wrote four more books!

Soon after the war ended, the family came back to Australia to settle in Mabel Street in Traralgon, close to Mary's brother Maxwell, and their parents. Although not wealthy, they did employ a cook and a maid. Mary hated domestic drudgery! They mixed in local affairs. They camped in the South Gippsland hills. They went to Eden for holidays. In 1925 a week-long Back-to-Sale was organized. Mary and George took Mary's father, Lewis, now widowed. They all had a whale of a time! Mary continued to turn out books; she encouraged women's organisations in Gippsland, such as the Fellowship of Gippsland Women; she often appeared in local towns to support charitable work. For a short time she took a job in Melbourne as editor of *Women's World*. Mary enjoyed one side of women's new-found freedoms – she smoked up to forty cigarettes a day!

In 1927 the family returned to Britain. Despite Mary's rosy outlook of a few years earlier, they found it impossible to live in Cork because of the sectarian bitterness – indeed, dangers – into which Ireland had now plunged. Accordingly, the family went, unwillingly, to a country house near Omagh in Ulster (Northern Ireland). Jon, in true Billabong fashion, went to board at Repton, one of the great English Public Schools. Sadly, Patrick, the younger son, died in a shooting accident two years after their arrival. He was twelve years old. Deeply grieving, Mary and George left Ireland, and there followed a long period – from 1929 to 1939 – when they lived at Bexhill-on-Sea in East Sussex, although during this time they travelled quite a lot on the Continent.

In 1939, after a twelve-year absence, Mary and George made a triumphant return to Melbourne, ostensibly to settle Jon on his farm at Beaconsfield Upper. Their arrival on the new glamour liner, the Dominion Monarch, was trumpeted in every newspaper in the country. Receptions were held for them in Perth and in Adelaide as the liner put in there. In Melbourne there was a civic reception in the Town Hall given by the Lady Mayoress. They were invited to attend functions so often Mary quipped that they could be said to be 'eating their way around Australia'. Mary threw herself into a round of charitable and fund-raising appearances. At schools she would be presented with illuminated addresses. At hospital appearances her signed books would be offered as prizes. In Sale the Mayor tended her a civic reception. Mary spoke warmly about her old home town, as the Gippsland Times reported:

She had seen a good deal since she left Sale but in all her travels Sale had been the heart of the world to her. She recalled her school days here when she used to ride her pony about Sale, fish for eels in the Lake and sit on the steps at the Library absorbed in a book. She thought Sale was favoured in having such a good library. She had a reading permit when she was eight years of age. In all her work, her schooling at Sale and her environment here had been the background. The advancement the town had made pleased her very much and she hoped it would continue to prosper. She thanked the Mayor for his kindness in thus enabling her to meet so many old friends.

Grant Bruce seems to have become increasingly conservative in her views. In the 'thirties, having visited Italy, she spoke favourably of Mussolini:

Mussolini is an intense force underlying or overtopping the whole national life. His rule is as drastic as his reforms, but his followers adore him, and would die for him to a man. He has put down night clubs because he says the young manhood of the nation cannot work if it dissipates its strength in such ways, and he is fighting immorality tooth and nail. One of his latest restrictions is that no lease can be issued for a house or flat unless the tenants produce a marriage certificate.

Inevitably times change and some of the views expressed in her books are now seen as outmoded, especially regarding racial stereotypes and the place of aborigines in society. Recent editions of her Billabong books have been edited to avoid controversy.

In later years, in Australia, Grant Bruce, now in her 'sixties, became more didactic, more inclined to want to shape others towards her own predilections – and always with an eye to improving the nation as a whole. Thus, this report of Grant Bruce speaking to the Dandenong CWA in 1940:

In these troubled times of public anxiety and with our own individual crosses to bear, we needed something more than human strength to help us meet the present, and face the future. A way to obtain this added courage was to analyse our thoughts and to realise how they affect us. During one period in her own life she had experienced a very tragic happening and reverse after reverse had followed. At that time, she and her husband came into contact with a friend from the East, who was filled with great wisdom. ... He introduced to them a system that helped them marvellously. It was deep breathing in a certain manner, coupled with thought. As one breathed, every cell of the lungs was used. As you inhaled you held the thought of courage; as you exhaled you cast out the opposite thought—fear. They practised this system, and within a month began to feel a difference in health. ... Fear was banished .and she had gained confidence. Many of us fear worries that never materialise, and we should find an avenue of escape. ... We should find a way of schooling ourselves to win a way to serenity and happiness.

The Second World War aroused all Grant Bruce's national sympathies. She wrote extensively and broadcast frequently in support of the war effort. She pleaded with her audiences to put money into War Saving Certificates; she praised schools where the children were raising money for war needs; she told uplifting stories of life in London during the Blitz; she urged austerity at all levels, and all with a heavy tinge of moral persuasion:

Make it easy for your friends to economise by stating frankly that you're going to do it. Let them know that you're more interested in helping to end the war than in spending on oddments — and therefore your money is going into war funds .... I think you'll be surprised to find how many will gladly follow your lead. Each person you influence will become another centre for the same influence: the movement goes on, spreading like ripples of water, becoming more powerful than you can imagine. And you'll have the satisfaction of knowing two things - that you've backed up the men who are giving their lives for you, and that you've helped others to take the only line of conduct that can ease our minds to-day.

The outbreak of war soon after their arrival put paid to Mary's hopes of a settled life in her home country. Mary and George went to Beaconsfield Upper with their son, Jon, and his family, although soon afterwards Jon joined up and went overseas on military service. Mary did a good deal of war work. Apart from the radio broadcasts and written articles for the Department of Information, she worked for the AIF Women's Association and supported charity functions where, for instance, she would sell her autograph for sixpence to raise funds. In 1942 came her last book, *BillabongRiders* – the last of thirty-eight altogether. In 1949 George died and Mary went to live in Melbourne. In 1952 she visited England once more, but soon returned. She was unsettled and feeling her age. According to one of her biographers, Alison Alexander, she hated the thought of people seeing her deteriorate and so returned to England where she was less well known. She died there in 1958, aged eighty.

As life went on, Mary found herself growing more and more away from the kind of life she was depicting in her published works. As Alison Alexander has observed:

The author of books extolling the conventional way of life was herself very unconventional; the inventor of the tomboyish yet feminine Norah was an enthusiastic feminist; the extoller of country life actually disliked it, preferring a city; and the creator of the all-Australian Linton family lived a large part of her life overseas and thought of herself as partly Irish.

The Mary Grant Bruce memorial in Sale, installed in 2011, a hundred years after Mary's first book was published, has the inscription:

Mary Grant Bruce 1878 - 1958

Renowned children's author.

Particularly remembered for her "Billabong" series of books, made a major contribution towards building an Australian self image.

Born and schooled in Sale. Life long association with Gippsland.

SIR FRANK MACFARLANE BURNET

... who spent his childhood in Traralgon and became the foremost scientist of his time.

Frank Macfarlane Burnet was, by most reckonings, Australia's pre-eminent man of science.

At home he is best remembered as a crusading Director of the Walter and Eliza Hall Institute and as the first Australian of the Year. He is also one of the few who have been made a Knight of the Order of Australia. Internationally he is known as a Nobel Prize winning virologist who laid a foundation for the modern application of immunology in many fields of medicine.

Macfarlane Burnet spent his boyhood in Traralgon, the son of a bank manager in town. He was born here in the last days of the nineteenth century, on 3 September, 1899, and moved away ten years later when his father was transferred to Terang in the Western District of Victoria. He went to a private infant school for a short time, but spent most of his Traralgon years at the State School. Those years stayed with him all his life, especially the time he spent along the banks of the Traralgon Creek. In a letter written from the middle of a bleak London winter many years later, he recalled:

...the view up to the Callignee hills along the creek. ... It's a particularly attractive place to me ... all my memories are romantic ones of a small boy ... I'd love to show you where I once caught an eel in my hand [and] where I used to catch mussels by pushing a reed into their open mouths in the mud of the creek bottom.

However, Burnet was not one to romanticise his childhood – nor anything else in life. When he looked back on his early years, he detected in himself the signs of the man he was to become. In his book, *Changing Patterns*, he writes how research scientists often display typical characteristics in childhood. He quotes with approval the words of clinical psychologist, Ann Roe, that those who pursue a career in research science are "socially late-maturing boys *[sic]* with strong hobbies and noticeable persistence in them. ... [They are] voracious if unselective readers. ...Most regarded their fathers with great respect but felt somewhat distant from them."

Burnet reveals a lot about himself here. In fact, he was out of tune with many of his father's attitudes and activities. For instance, his father was a sportsman, playing golf and fishing; his son showed no interest in sport. His father attended church, yet mixed freely with non-churchmen; his son thought this hypocritical. Burnet the boy did read whatever he could lay his hands on, especially science fiction ... and as for hobbies, he had an insatiable interest in beetles, an interest he carried into his adult years. His beetle collection was enormous. "I was a biologist at birth," he once commented.

As a boy and throughout his life Burnet was always known as 'Mac'. He was the second child of seven. His older sister, Doris, had a mental condition which meant that there were seldom visitors to the family home. As well, Mac's mother was dominated by the need to care for her daughter. As a result, Burnet grew up without close support from either of his parents and engrossed in his own interests rather than mixing freely with others of his own age. We see here, I believe, the seeds of the future leader, who tended to act without consulting his colleagues. He earned their respect, but not the warmth of their companionship.

In Terang, Burnet revelled in the outdoor life, especially around Lake Terang and at Port Fairy, where the family took their annual holidays. His reading expanded as did his beetle collection. Later in life, Burnet was to eschew religious belief, but in Terang he attended the Presbyterian Church with his family. At the end of his primary schooling at the local state school, he won a full boarding scholarship to Geelong College. It was not a happy time for the bookish boy in the robust company of the other boarders. However he put a bold face on it and emerged as dux of the school as well as topping most of the subjects in his final year.

He was now seventeen and the year was 1916. The Great War was in mid-course. Australian troops had suffered defeat at Gallipoli and were now immersed in the horrors of the Western Front. Burnet had a fundamental distaste for war and chose to study medicine because, it has been said, it would make it more likely that in the event of his being called into military service he would be given non-combat duties. Accordingly, he began his medical studies at Melbourne University at the beginning of 1917, again being awarded a full residential scholarship at Ormond College.

Burnet was happier at university where his fellow-students were more understanding of his distinctive personality (and also of his beetle collection!) Amazingly, he won a place in Ormond's 1st VIII rowing crew. Again, he topped many of his courses and sometimes found it more profitable to miss some lectures to study on his own. In his third year, when clinical work began, his taste for research rather than diagnostic work became evident. Besides, his abrupt manner was not conducive to a good bedside persona. After once more graduating brilliantly he was given a residency at the Melbourne Hospital (later the Royal Melbourne), but he continued to lean towards laboratory work and moved from his hospital work to a senior residency in pathology at the Walter and Eliza Hall Institute of Research in Parkville.

His abilities quickly becoming apparent, it was next arranged for Burnet to spend two years at the Lister Institute of Preventive Medicine in London, where he completed his PhD. On return he was made Assistant Principal of the Walter and Eliza Hall Institute. In the same year, 1928, Burnet married Linda Druce (in the Presbyterian Church in Kew!) In that same year, a terrible tragedy occurred in Bundaberg, Queensland. Twenty-one children became seriously ill after being inoculated for diphtheria. Twelve died. The subsequent Royal Commission delegated much of the pathological work to Macfarlane Burnet, who was able to establish that the batch of inoculant had been contaminated by a golden staph toxin. The tragedy brought national and international recognition for both Burnet himself and the Walter and Eliza Hall Institute.

I am now going to follow (and simplify) Sir Gustav Nossal's account of Macfarlane Burnet's career in science. It may not do justice to the extent of his brilliance, but I hope I can make it understandable to lay folk like myself. After four years in Melbourne, Burnet was offered a fellowship to work once more in London with the National Institute for Medical Research. For the next two years he was engaged in work in the field of virology. Little was then known of the effect of viruses on human or animal health. Burnet then returned to Melbourne, to the Walter and Eliza Hall Institute, and spent the next quarter of a century extending human understanding of this aspect of medicine.

His first solid body of work dealt with bacteriophage viruses, tiny parasites that infect and grow within bacteria. Using laboratory animals, Burnet studied how invisible virus particles attached themselves to the bacterial host cell and how they grew inside it, finally bursting the cell and releasing a brood of progeny into the growth medium. He noted how the genetic material of the virus appeared to integrate with the genetic material of the bacterium, and how certain processes could extract it again, activating viral growth. He was ahead of his time. Overseas, others built on his work, laying the foundations of our modern understanding of how microbes grow and mutate, and how they can be controlled.

In 1944, now aged in his mid-forties, Burnet was appointed Director of the Walter and Eliza Hall Institute, turning down the offer of a chair at Harvard in favour of his Melbourne appointment. At the same time, he was appointed Professor of Experimental Medicine at Melbourne University. Burnet and his team, though small by international reckoning, had become world leaders in the field of virology.

His first major contribution to the field of animal viruses was to improve and elaborate on the technique of growing these organisms in fertile hens' eggs. Burnet worked out how simple mouth or nasal washings could be injected into eggs as a convenient way of isolating a fresh virus. He learnt how to grow large quantities of a virus in this way. The present method of producing enough influenza virus to mass-produce vaccines is based on this work. Burnet also carried out important studies into poliomyelitis. His work also covered many types of pox, including cowpox and mousepox, herpes; mumps, psittacosis and many other viruses and bacteria. His initial discovery of the influenza virus was light-heartedly described in the irreverent Melbourne journal, *Smith's Weekly*:

On a grey day in 1933, a young Melbourne scientist associated with the research staff at the National Health and Medical Research Institute, Hampstead (Eng.), experienced one of his most thrilling moments. What was there to be thrilled about? A FERRET SNEEZED! Well, the nasal organisms of a ferret have characteristics similar, in some degree, to those of humans. And this ferret was one of several that had been injected with an influenza virus. So Dr. Frank M. Burnet, now Director of the Walter and Eliza Hall Institute, of Melbourne, knew by this sneeze that he had reached an important goal — the discovery of the virus of influenza and the common cold.

Despite the complexity of Burnet's work, it relied on simple methods of trial and observation. Nossal puts it this way:

Burnet's was a contemplative, almost a solitary, kind of genius. The majority of his papers were single-author works, using simple, elegant techniques, frequently of his own devising and requiring little more than a Pasteur pipette, a test tube, a fertile hen's egg and a microscope.

Burnet sought to get close to the nature of viral reproduction, and thus to the secret of life. He made use of the membranes surrounding the chick embryo to develop a new method of quantifying virus numbers, giving his research a precision never before encountered. In 1951 Burnet and a co-worker found that when a cell was infected with two different influenza virus strains, some of the progeny viruses that resulted recombined with traits of each of the parent strains. It is now known that such viruses can lead to the outbreak of major epidemics. Often his findings led to immediate application to real-life situations. Such was his team's discovery of the cause of 'Q' fever in abattoir workers and the production of a vaccine to control it. At another time, he worked with Jean MacNamara in establishing that there were two distinct types of polio virus, which led to different kinds of vaccines being used to overcome this disease, so common in the 'thirties and 'forties.

In 1951, a public outcry occurred when it was claimed that the current outbreak of Murray Valley encephalitis in Northern Victoria was linked to the widespread use of myxomotosis in the control of rabbits. Burnet argued against the link and, in order to demonstrate the truth of his assertion, he injected himself, together with two other notable scientists, Dr Frank Fenner and Dr Ian Clunies-Ross, with enough myxomotosis virus to kill more than a hundred rabbits. There were no ill-effects. When the minister for the CSIRO announced the result in Federal Parliament there were cheers throughout the House.

In 1957 Burnet dropped something of a bombshell in unilaterally announcing that henceforth the Walter and Eliza Hall Institute would cease all work on virology and devote itself entirely to immunology. Many of the Institute's staff saw this as arrogance and, indeed, wrong. Many left, most going to the ANU's School of Medical Research. However, Burnet's own research work continued to prosper. In 1960 he was awarded, as co-recipient with a Brazilian-English scientist, Peter Medawar, the Nobel Prize for Physiology or Medicine. The award was for providing the experimental basis for inducing immune tolerance, which in turn led to the ability to transplant organs in humans and animals. Most of Burnet's work was theoretical, opening the way for others to proceed. "My part in the discovery of acquired immunological tolerance was a very minor one," he once commented. "It was the formulation of an hypothesis that called for experiment."

In a speech to Swedish university students on the occasion of the award of his Nobel Prize, Burnet revealed some broader sympathies than were apparent in his everyday work:

... For all of us this is probably the greatest day of our lives – and for myself it has a special significance. I have come to this celebration from a greater distance than any previous laureate and as the first Australian to appear on the Nobel list. I think that this occasion has a rather special significance for my own country, a middling small country a little bigger than Sweden but only now beginning to create an image of its own in the eyes of the world. Some day I hope that we will take our place along with Sweden as one of the centres where knowledge can go along with social progress to the good life we all seek. ... To advance science is highly honourable. ... But other things are equally honourable and perhaps when you are 20-30 years older, research as we know it, may be less important than it is today. Today and always there will be an obligation to pass on to the new generation the tradition of liberal scholarship – scientific or in the humanities – and to bring the understanding of things and human actions to everyone.

Despite the Nobel Prize being given for Burnet's work in immune tolerance, in scientific circles Burnet is best remembered for his clonal selection theory, in which he predicted almost all the features of the immune system as understood today. The best summary of this theory is in Wendy Lewis's 2010 book, *Australians of the Year*, which I've followed here. The key problem in immunology during the 1940s and 1950s was to explain how the human body produced so many different antibodies to fight various kinds of infection. Following up earlier work by Jerne and Talmadge, Burnet proposed that the immune system generates a large number of white blood cells that are all different. When a white blood cell meets a specific foreign invader it reacts in two ways: it fights the invader and it clones itself to make more white blood cells to fight the infection. The foundation of this theory - that is, that a single white blood cell makes only a single type of antibody – was verified in later studies. More than 20 years later Jerne wrote:

the enormous advances since 1957 in our knowledge of the immune system have proved Burnet's hypothesis to be basically correct even in its very first formulation. ... In summary I hit the nail, but then he hit the nail on its head.

Burnet believed himself that he should have received the Nobel Prize for this work rather than for the work actually rewarded in 1960.

After 1960, and now in his 'sixties, Burnet scaled back his research work to concentrate on writing. He was also taken up more with administration. The Institute was expanded. Burnet's view remained, however, that to be most effective a research institute should be small enough to be controlled by the single figure at the head of it. He continued to fit this description, deciding the Institute's policies and personally selecting all the research staff and students. In 1965 he retired, to be succeeded as Director by another scientist of international repute, Sir Gus Nossal. A later (1994) reviewer of Burnet's direction of the institute described the Institute under his leadership as 'probably the world's best-known research centre devoted to the study of immunology', but noted that with increasing sophistication in medical science, Burnet's lone-wolf approach became less compatible with the research environment which required more collaboration.

In the later stages of his career and in his retirement, Burnet began to write more popular works on subjects like human biology, cancer, and ageing. Thirteen books appeared in a dozen years. Many were translated into other languages. He took a particular interest in ageing. His view was that personal characteristics rather than organic health were more important than usually allowed for. In particular he believed that job satisfaction was a key element in a continuing healthy old age. He published his views in his book, *Endurance of Life*, where he argued that there was a physiological basis for job satisfaction increasing longevity. However, he stepped into dangerous territory when he went on to argue that innate differences between men and women - aggression tendencies, for example - were genetic in nature and not capable of being overcome. Further, he argued for the legalisation of euthanasia and also of compassionate infanticide in the case of children in utero or born with overwhelming disabilities. A public storm ensued. Burnet defended his views: *The aim is entirely humanitarian - to spare the child of a short, painful and meaningless life and to alleviate the mental agony of the parents.* In his older age, Burnet became quite pessimistic about the ability of society as a whole to improve intellectually or physically.

This survey of the work of Sir Frank Macfarlane Burnet has only scratched the surface of his vast contribution to scientific and medical research. A list of the principal honours extended to him would include the following: he was knighted in the New Year's Honours list in 1951, he received the Elizabeth II Coronation Medal in 1953, and was appointed to the Order of Merit (OM) in the 1958 Queen's Birthday Honours List. In 1960 he was the first recipient of the Australian of the Year award. He was appointed Knight Commander of the Order of the British Empire (KBE) in the 1969 New Year Honours list, and received the Elizabeth II Jubilee Medal in 1977. In 1978 he was made a Knight of the Order of Australia (AK).

He was a fellow or honorary member of thirty international Academies of Sciences and the American Philosophical Society. He received ten honorary D.Sc. degrees from universities including Harvard, Cambridge and Oxford, and honorary doctorates from several other universities in Australia and overseas. Including his Nobel Prize, he received nineteen medals or awards, including the Royal Medal and the Copley Medal from the Royal Society. He also took up a total of thirty-three international lectureships and seventeen lectureships within Australia.

After his death, Australia's largest communicable diseases research institute—the Macfarlane Burnet Centre for Medical Research - was renamed in his honour. The Burnet Clinical Research Unit of the Walter and Eliza Hall Institute was also named in his recognition in 1986. His work on immunology has been recognised on several occasions by the issue of stamps by Australia Post.

In 1978, now aged seventy-eight, Burnet finally put up his pen. His first wife, Linda, had died five years earlier after forty years of marriage. During her final years, Burnet refused all offers of lectures overseas to spend more time nursing his ailing wife. For a time after this he became very reclusive. He moved into Ormond College for company and resumed beetle collecting. Gradually he regained his enthusiasm and began writing again. In 1975, he travelled to California to deliver a series of lectures. Then, in 1976 he married Hazel Jenkins, a widow who was working in the microbiology department as a librarian and moved out of Ormond College.

He died of cancer in 1985, aged eighty-five, while staying with his son in Port Fairy and was buried in the local cemetery. In 1999 the people of Traralgon erected a fine bust of Sir Frank in bronze outside the town's Post Office. The inscription reads:

Sir Macfarlane Burnet
OM., AK., KBE
Born Traralgon 3. 9. 1899
Died 31.8.1985

Awarded Nobel Prize for Medicine 1960

HELEN CALDICOTT

... one of the world's leading anti-nuclear campaigners, who mixed with international leaders, and chose to live in Gippsland in later years.

When I was nineteen, I read a book that changed my life. It was a novel, barely read these days, called On the Beach, by the Australian writer Nevil Shute. ... It tells the story of the final months in the lives of five people living in a world doomed to be destroyed by radiation after a nuclear war that had begun by accident in the Northern Hemisphere.... Shute's story haunted me. Millions of words have since been written about nuclear war and its consequences, and much of the literature is more horrific and emotive than anything Nevil Shute wrote or perhaps even imagined. But his novel was set in Melbourne, the city where I had grown up. It described places I knew, devastated by nuclear catastrophe. Nowhere was safe. I felt so alone, so unprotected by the adults, who seemed to be unaware of the danger.... after reading On the Beach, I knew I wouldn't just go through medical school and settle into a nice, cosy, well-paid niche somewhere, as doctors in Australia were apt to do. I wanted a husband and a family, certainly, but somewhere in me was a conviction that I had other work to do as well.

Helen Caldicott thus describes the epiphany that led to a lifetime of making people 'aware of the danger' of nuclear devastation.

Originally Helen Broinowski, she was brought up in Melbourne, went to public schools and to Fintona, where she is remembered by classmates as 'the girl who kept on asking questions'. Helen went on to do medicine in Adelaide. She graduated in 1961 and married her paediatrician-husband William soon after. For a time, though still nursing her passion in the anti-nuclear field, she pursued a normal, though distinguished, career in paediatrics. After a three-year stint at Harvard, Helen returned to Adelaide's Queen Elizabeth Hospital as Director of the renal unit. Six months after she began working there, she pricked her finger on a contaminated needle, contracted hepatitis, and nearly died. However, she found further inspiration for her life's work in the incident. "Like many people who have faced death, you feel you've been saved for something," she said later. "Life becomes a gift. There had to be a reason why you didn't die then."

After further studies Caldicott qualified as a paediatric physician and established Australia's first cystic fibrosis clinic at the Adelaide Children's Hospital. From 1977 to 1980 she was in Boston, teaching at the Boston Children's Hospital Medical Centre and at Harvard Medical School. However, all this time Helen Caldicott's mind had been running on those other things – that 'other work' to alert the world to the horrors of nuclear war and the dangers of a nuclear arms build-up. As one reviewer has put it, 'to prevent 'On the Beach' from becoming reality'.

It was the French government's testing of nuclear weapons in the Pacific that brought Caldicott's first foray into the public arena. In 1971, news broke that the French had been secretly testing nuclear bombs in the atmosphere in the Mururoa Atoll in the South Pacific, contrary to international agreement. Her letter to an Adelaide newspaper exposing this action catapulted Caldicott into the forefront of the impassioned nuclear debate that ensued. At about the same time a report indicated that Adelaide's drinking water contained nuclear fall-out. Australian national and environmental instincts were aroused. Widespread demonstrations followed. French goods were boycotted. Postal workers refused to deliver mail from France. The anti-nuclear, anti-French campaign, headed by Caldicott, played a part in the election of Gough Whitlam's Labor government the following year, 1972. Australian exports of uranium were eventually stopped by Trade Union action, while the French government gave up atmospheric nuclear testing under Australian and international pressure.

Helen Caldicott had played a major role in the actions of the unions and of the Federal government. She proved to be a brilliant and persuasive communicator. Speaking to Trade Unionists in Australia at the time of the French nuclear tests, she converted their hesitancy into action by tailoring her address to things close to their hearts. "I would convince them in ten minutes," said Caldicott. "I just talked about the effect ... on their testicles and what radiation does to the genes and sperm, and I'd talk about nuclear war and what it means to their children."

Helen Caldicott had become a household name. Shortly afterwards, the Caldicott family moved once more to Boston. Helen remained consumed in the anti-nuclear field, at some cost to family togetherness. William had to undertake much of the care of the three children. Family harmony was tided over at that point, though William was to leave the marriage later on. Life for Helen had become a non-stop cavalcade of public lectures, TV appearances, cross-country flights, and commentary on matters to do with nuclear energy at any time of day or night. In a podcast recorded in 2023 she recalled those days of frenetic activity:

I had a wonderful agent.... She would get me on television, not as this boring old Australian doctor talking about nuclear power and boring the hell out of people ... She put me in Vogue and Life & Time and Family Circle. So the average Joe with his six-pack sitting back with his family at night watching television learned about the dangers of nuclear war and by the end of the 80s I was all over the place, I'd go to three cities a day – address 1000 people and then get the plane and go somewhere else and do the same thing.

Her style of presentation is neatly expressed in this comment about her 1982 documentary, *If You Love This Planet:*

It features an attractive, elegantly dressed woman, with auburn hair and intense pale-blue eyes delivering one of her typically shocking, scientifically precise, medically accurate, and emotional speeches about exactly what happens when a nuclear bomb lands on your city.

Amidst her constant speaking and writing, Helen swung her energy into the moribund organization, Physicians for Social Responsibility (PSR), which grew to a membership of 23,000 members and became one of the principal anti-nuclear organisations in the United States. Caldicott was the initial President, from 1978 until 1984. By coincidence, the Society's first public press notice coincided with the disastrous meltdown of a reactor at the Three Mile Island nuclear power plant in Massachusetts, releasing radio-active gases and radio-active iodine into the environment. It remains the worst accident in US commercial power plant history. The PSR rode the crest of the popular anti-nuclear sentiment that consumed the country. Caldicott became the foremost voice in anti-nuclear politics in the USA.

She believed strongly that it was through women that a basic change in attitudes towards the dangers of nuclear warfare would be brought about. In her public addresses she appealed particularly to women and to feminine instincts of preservation and security. Recently, she commented:

So we're in the hands of un-informed - not ill-informed – un-informed people, mostly men, and that really irritates me. Because the fact is that 52% of the population is women. We have hormones to nurture life, oxytocin, estrogen, progesterone, and men have testosterone, and we are in the hands of men. Why do we allow that to happen?

In 1980 she founded Women's Action for Nuclear Disarmament (WAND) - now re-named Women's Action for New Directions - which, together with PSR, has remained a very influential lobby group for the cause of nuclear disarmament. Caldicott also found time to travel to other countries, spreading the word and founding similar organisations to the PSR in England, Ireland, Scotland, Holland, Germany, Belgium, Scandinavia, Canada, Japan, New Zealand, and here at home in Australia.

Caldicott had an hour-long meeting with the US President of the time, Ronald Reagan. Any hopes she had of influencing his conservative policies in a non-nuclear direction were soon quashed. "It was the most shocking experience of my life," she commented. "You expect the President to be intelligent and well-informed. I found the opposite … Everything he said to me was inaccurate." Nevertheless, largely because of the Three Mile Island episode rather than through a change in government attitudes, the nuclear power industry was scaled back considerably in the US.

With the re-election of Reagan in 1984, conservative forces in USA were re-generated against the 'left-wing' policies of Caldicott and the anti-nuclear movement. Her opponents linked her with Communist elements in the nation. She came under constant personal attack. Her critics accused her of using alarmist methods and a lack of thorough research. It is true to say that Caldicott was an educator and communicator rather than a researcher in the field of atomic energy and application.

In a state of exhaustion, Caldicott resigned from the PSR and also announced that she would give up her anti-nuclear campaigning. She began to channel her energies more into the environmental movement generally rather than into the more specific anti-nuclear field. At about that time there was a significant development in her whole outlook on life. Raised as an agnostic, she was for many years an atheist, but became a non-sectarian believer in God as the life force of the universe. 'Now I believe God is life, the DNA molecule, reality,' she wrote. 'Prayer gives me strength. I know I'm on the side of truth, that I'm doing the right thing, and that inspires me.' Then came a positive and personally rewarding moment. In 1985, the Nobel Peace Prize was awarded to a confederation of peace organisations, Caldicott's Physicians for Social Responsibility being prominent amongst them. The award was given 'for spreading authoritative information and by creating awareness of the catastrophic consequences of nuclear war'.

Soon afterwards, the Caldicott family returned to Australia, settling at first in the NSW coastal town of Bermagui. For a brief time Caldicott became involved directly in political activity in the hope of achieving her environmental ambitions. She founded the Green Labor Party within the Australian Labor Party. Green Labor stood for closing down American bases in Australia, banning visits by nuclear-powered ships, the abolition of uranium mining and wood-chipping, as well as limiting population growth. Caldicott believed that most politicians were scientifically illiterate and that independent thinkers, especially those with a scientific background, were needed to run for government.

For the Federal election of 1990, however, Caldicott moved to Byron Bay and was persuaded to stand for the seat of Richmond in northern New South Wales as an Independent. The seat had been in the hands of the Country Party, later the National Party, since 1922 and was held by the Leader of the Nationals at the time, Charles Blunt. In a 2021 interview she looked back on the circumstances:

There was such enthusiasm, such a sense of relief in the electorate – crowded halls of people everywhere. I think it solidified most people's ideas on the dangers of nuclear and global warming; they were so relieved to be represented.

Caldicott polled 23.3% of the vote, and her preferences pushed the Labor candidate across the line. It was just the second time a sitting party leader had been defeated in Australian political history.

The early 1990s were turbulent years for Caldicott. In 1992, she published an important and influential book, *If you love this Planet*. At the same time she became interested in the 'All One Voice' movement. All One Voice sought to establish communities of peace-loving, environmentally-conscious people in rural areas. They developed a life-style that included bartering, permaculture, and developing energy from wind and solar sources. At the same time there was an educational and missional aspect of their work. Classes were held for members and for people in the general community. Many people were attracted to the movement.

This is where Caldicott's Gippsland connection comes in. She moved to Brandy Creek, a short distance from both Drouin and Warragul. Brandy Creek is a historic village, the earliest settlement in the area, and an important point on the oldest land route into Gippsland, the Old Sale Road. Caldicott lived in one of the pioneer cottages there, unbeknownst to most of the people in the district. Warragul became the focus point of the local All One Voice movement. The group took over the White House, one of the premier buildings in the town. Classes in environmental and related matters were held there and in other places such as the Community College. Caldicott was heavily involved in these classes. Several people moved to the district, attracted by the presence of the movement. Although active within All One Voice, Caldicott did not become personally well-known in the wider community.

Next, Caldicott moved to Koonwarra in South Gippsland. Here the movement bought a shop doubling as a café providing organic meals and selling organic produce to the public. The movement also received a strong following in Leongatha. Followers were encouraged to establish healthy businesses, such as nurseries, and to reach out into the community. Although All One Voice is inactive in the Gippsland community now, its influence remains. The 'back-to-earth' followers, especially in South Gippsland, could trace the growth of their movement back to the impetus given by Caldicott and those around her who championed organic produce and the bringing together of sympathetic people.

Caldicott appears to have become disenchanted with the All One Voice movement. By the middle-'nineties, she had moved away, and since then has spent her time between her home in New York and here in Australia. She continues to write and broadcast. She describes herself as 'global physician' or a 'planetary physician'.

Helen Caldicott is widely recognised as one of the most significant women of the modern era. She has been awarded twenty-one honorary doctoral degrees, and in 1982 the Humanist of the Year award from the American Humanist Association. In 1992, she received the Peace Abbey Courage of Conscience Award at the John F. Kennedy Presidential Library in Boston. Her name was placed on the Victorian Honour Roll of Women in 2001. She was awarded the Lannan Foundation Prize for Cultural Freedom in 2003, and in 2006, the Peace Organisation of Australia presented her with the inaugural Australian Peace Prize "for her longstanding commitment to raising awareness about the medical and environmental hazards of the nuclear age". The Smithsonian Institution has named her as one of the most influential women of the 20th century. She is a member of the scientific committee of the Fundacion Ideas, a progressive think tank in Spain.

In 2009 Caldicott was designated a Women's History Month Honoree by the National Women's History Project. Five decades of her work regarding the dangers of nuclear weapons are honoured and recognized by the US Peace Memorial Foundation in its *US Peace Registry*. Among dozens of other awards, I might mention particularly the Thomas Merton Prize for Peace and the Gandhi Peace Prize. Above all, there is the Nobel Peace Prize of 1985, given to an umbrella of peace organisations centred on Caldicott, as mentioned above.

Caldicott has also produced and/or been the subject of numerous documentaries and films. Her short film, *If you love this Planet*, won the Academy Award for Best Short Documentary, 1982. Caldicott was the subject of an award-winning documentary, *Helen's War: Portrait of a Dissident* (2004), made by her niece, Anna Broinowski. The film, *Eight Minutes to Midnight*, by Mary Benjamin, was nominated for an Academy Award in 1981. Many documentaries by and about Caldicott are freely available on the internet.

Dr Caldicott has written, co-written, or edited more than a dozen books. The most significant, probably, are *Nuclear Madness* (1978), the pamphlet, *Towards a Compassionate Society* (1991), *If you love this Planet* (1992), *War in Heaven* (2007), *Sleepwalking to Armageddon* (2017), and her autobiography, *A Desperate*

Passion (1996). A portrait of Dr Caldicott by Leeanne Crisp (2021) hangs in the National Gallery, Canberra.

Helen Caldicott is still as driven and as expressive as she ever was. Take these excerpts, the first from 2020:

Seventy-five years after the dawn of the nuclear age, we are as ready as ever to extinguish ourselves. The human race is clearly an evolutionary aberrant on a suicidal mission. Our planet is in the intensive care unit, approaching several terminal events. Will we gradually burn and shrivel life on our wondrous Earth by emitting the ancient carbon stored over billions of years to drive our cars and power our industries, or will we end it suddenly by creating a global gas oven?

And from 2022:

What we desperately need is a global resolution to coordinate and reach out to all nations, to live in peace and stop the killing, and to feed the millions of starving children in Yemen and other countries in desperate need of food. In other words, practice global preventive medicine to save the planetary population and the wondrous species that co-habit the globe with us.

And in 2023, she showed that she still has fire in her belly. Following a showing of one of her films, she said in an interview:

I'm a paediatrician, specialist in the environment, because the earth is in great danger and I want to preserve life on earth for the rest of time. That's what I do. I practise global preventive medicine.

... Tony Guterres, the Secretary-General of the United Nations said the other day that we are one miscalculation away from nuclear annihilation because the military and the military industrial complex in America are now putting their weapons under the control of artificial intelligence, that within ten years artificial intelligence control of nuclear weapons will make nuclear war a certainty. Why are they doing it? God only knows!

... It is imperative that we understand, because, as President Jefferson said, an informed democracy will perform in a responsible fashion, and at the moment this democracy – America, and Australia and globally – is totally ill informed or uninformed about these notions that will destroy all of us in a flash. And remember that the politicians are not our leaders. We are the leaders. They are our representatives and we must make sure they represent us.

The world is on hair-trigger alert and we go about our daily lives not even understanding. Can you think of anything more evil? - and it all happens behind our backs and it all happens using American hard-earned tax dollars that should be going to education, the environment and the like. ... In a nuclear war, no one will survive. There will be no one to reproduce and have babies, and what's more, almost all the animals on earth will be killed. What's more, all the wonderful plant species, the wonder of evolution and of nature, the brilliance of evolution, will be destroyed.

Having watched this film and having taken in all the information you've just heard, I want you to go out into your garden or into the park and go and smell the flowers. And go and watch the bees and the butterflies and realise how extraordinary it is – the profusion of nature, and how much you love your children and what a privilege it is that you were ever born into existence. Then you will rise up and decide you've got to save your children, the butterflies, and bees, the birds, the flowers ... if you love this planet, ... and I'm sure you do, ... if you love yourself ...!

GRACE JENNINGS CARMICHAEL

... the 'sweet singer of Orbost' who wrote wonderful lyrical poetry, mixed with the leading writers of her day, moved to England, and died there in poverty in a London workhouse.

Grace Jennings Carmichael's earliest years were spent in Ballarat, but she moved to Orbost when she was a young girl, possibly when she was five, maybe when eight years old. Certainly her formative years were spent in Gippsland and it is the Gippsland bush that permeates her poems. Her mother had remarried after the death of Grace's father, and the little girl's step-father, Charles Henderson, was appointed manager of Sir William Clarke's Orbost Station on the outskirts of Orbost.

It is hard to find any personal or literary influence that might have inspired the young girl to begin writing. Rather, her parents frowned on her 'scribbling'. Consequently, she wrote her first poems hiding away in the forest and hid her work in a hollow tree before she went home. We could call her a real 'gumnut child'! Her best verses are about the sights and sounds and scents of the bush, profound because of their simplicity and honesty. Take this example:

Each soaring eucalypt, lifted high,

The wandering wind receives.

I watch the great boughs drawn against the sky,

Laden with trembling leaves.

A soft, harmonious music, full and rare,

Murmurs the boughs along –

The voice of Nature's God is solemn there,

In that deep undersong.

While still in her 'teens, she was bold enough to send a story to the *Bairnsdale Advertiser* which agreed to publish it. Thus encouraged, she submitted a poem to the *Weekly Times*, then, as now, a journal circulating mainly in the bush. Next, Carmichael tried the Melbourne weekly, the *Australasian*, a journal known to support emerging Australian writers. The first of her poems to be published in the *Australasian* was *The Old Maid*, which appeared in November, 1885. She was eighteen. The poem harks back to Carmichael's earliest days in Beaufort when her father was able to afford his family a more comfortable lifestyle than befell them in later years. The poem speaks of

> *Our calm old maid with the gentle eyes,*
> *And footstep soft and slow.*

The editor of the *Australasian*, David Watterston, was very encouraging. Over the years, most of her work was to appear in that journal under the name she used from then on for all her writing – simply 'Jennings Carmichael'. Maybe she chose to do this to disguise her gender!

When she was twenty Carmichael left Orbost and moved to Melbourne. Shortly afterwards she took up a position as a trainee nurse at the Melbourne Free Hospital for Sick Children in Rathdown Street, Carlton, which had been founded in 1870 'to help sick and injured children at no cost to families'. This charity hospital was the forerunner of the Royal Children's Hospital of today. A typhoid epidemic occurred at this time and Carmichael herself caught the disease and was off work, seriously ill, for a considerable time. However, she continued to write, much of it done to publicise the work being done at the hospital. In 1890 appeared her *Hospital Children*. It gathered together a number of pieces she had written previously as part of her attempts to bring the needs of the sick children to the attention and hearts of the general public.

Patricia Clarke, in her *Pen Portraits: Women Writers and Journalists in Nineteenth Century Australia*, has vividly described the nature of her work:

She wrote of a child victim of a "terrible hip disease" who wasted away "with blanched face and emaciated frame…until the cross of flowers is made for another childish figure in its mortuary shrouds"; of typhoid epidemics and of battered children: "...a dear little lad who recounted the history of certain bruises so reluctantly, and after entering into the details of flogging with a rope's end while strapped to a table, added wistfully – "But don't tell the other nurses; I don't want to disgrace my father". She wrote of child patients with hair so matted it had to be cut off, clothes so filthy they had to be burned and bodies so ingrained with dirt that they defied the best efforts with soap and water. She wrote also of the despair of seeing children return to hospital with a recurrence of illness after being neglected and allowed to roam cold, windy streets in ragged, thin clothing while their mothers were out earning a pittance washing, or out drinking.

A contemporary review in *Table Talk* gives a different view of Carmichael's writing:

She describes the scenes through which she has passed with such a winsome grace that, although there is no gainsaying the accuracy of her narration, she seems to divest it of all gloom and sadness. A hospital is not commonly associated with gaiety or lightness; there is too much pain and weariness to render the moral atmosphere very cheerful; but Miss Carmichael has the happy faculty of discovering the bright side of things in themselves clouded, and of practically demonstrating that there is a soul of goodness in things evil.

Her sketches about the hospital kept appearing in various newspapers and magazines. One was called *Christmas Day at the*

Children's Hospital, Melbourne, another, Hospital Mothers. The opening lines of this show something of Carmichael's style and sense of humour:

"What is the child's name?" "Sure, nurse, darlin', an' I forgit." "Do you not know your own child's name?" "Well, darlin', there's so many of 'em." The foregoing is the beginning of a dialogue between nurse and mother, which may be carried on in like fashion until the 'particulars' of the case are arrived at. The reader must imagine a highly-emotional daughter of Erin just parted from her offspring, whose frantic yells are probably resounding through the institution from an adjacent bathroom, where nurse is wrestling with young Australia. Between sympathy for her child and consideration for the nursing staff, the harassed woman is not in that state of mind best calculated to give any clear and trustworthy account of the patient's symptoms and condition generally. This woman kept reiterating, "Oh, nurse, darlin'; yes, darlin'," in a most idiotic fashion, her eyes roving meanwhile from the nurse's judicial countenance to the closed hall door. "He's a sensitive choild, darlin', an' may play up wid ye a bit. No, he weren't born in Victoria; it was in Collingwood— him and the two little 'uns." This conflicting statement was given with ominous interludes that foretold the explosion of true Irish grief, -which immediately followed. Nurse speaks a few words of practical but kindly sense, and the cross- examination continues, the soiled handkerchief

being kept in a convenient neighbourhood, meanwhile, in readiness for another eruption.

In 1890, now twenty-three, Carmichael qualified as a nurse and went to Geelong as a private nurse to a disabled boy who had artificial legs. She was now able to concentrate on her poetry. The first collection of her work was published in Melbourne and in England in 1895 under the simple title, *Poems*. The best of her poems spring from her upbringing in the deep forests of East Gippsland. One of the best known is *The Old Bush Road*, which carries the nostalgia of past times, yet on the sure foundations of sincerity and experience. It begins with gentle remembrance:

> *Dear old road, wheel-worn and broken,*
> *Winding through the forest green,*
> *Barred with shadows and with sunshine,*
> *Misty vistas drawn between.*
> *Grim, scarred bluegums ranged austerely,*
> *Lifting blackened columns each*
> *To the large, fair fields of azure,*
> *Stretching ever out of reach.*

Later in the poem, Carmichael turns to poignant regret of the old times passing:

Dear old road, no wonder, surely,
That I love thee like a friend!
And I grieve to think how surely
All thy loveliness will end.
For thy simple charm is passing,
And the turmoil of the street
Soon will mar thy sylvan silence
With the tramp of careless feet.

Responses to the publication of her first volume were generally favourable. One reviewer commented:

... Nature herself is looked at and described through the medium of womanly feeling. In other words, her inspiration is derived from her heart in a much greater degree than from her intellect, and for that very reason her poems will find a way into the appreciation of a far greater number of readers than if they dealt with abstractions, or social problems or classical myths ...Some of her landscape pictures are as good as anything of the kind yet produced by pen or pencil in this part of the world, ... it is "the still, sad music of humanity" which breaks through the great majority of the poems which will secure their acceptance on the part of the general public.

In April, 1895, Carmichael married an English architect, Francis Mullis, at the United Methodist Church in Fitzroy. She was twenty-eight, he thirty-five. Two years later the family moved to Adelaide. These years – the later years in Melbourne and the two years they were in Adelaide - were Carmichael's golden years. She was admitted to the Austral Salon in Collins Street, a club which brought together women to further literary and musical opportunities. She mixed and corresponded with other leading Australian literary figures and gave popular lectures on literary themes. This was in the day before modern outlets for mass entertainment existed, when public lectures were hugely popular. The first of these lectures was in Melbourne's Masonic Hall on 'The Spirit of the Bush', which became a favourite subject of Carmichael's in later lectures. Her talk was illustrated by music and song and the recitation of her poems. Alfred Deakin, later to be Prime Minister of Australia, was the Chairman.

After moving to Adelaide, her lectures continued. Her first appearance there was chaired by the Chief Justice of South Australia, and she added a second talk on 'Odd Little Mortals', no doubt reminiscing about her days at the Hospital for Sick Children. A reviewer commented that she "seemed to embody 'The Spirit of the Bush' in her own beautiful person". Major literary figures such as Henry Lawson were well-known to her. Lawson was later to write a moving tribute to her and her work.

Carmichael's first child was born in Adelaide, and shortly after the family sailed for England. Perhaps Mullis found the colonies too restricting, while Carmichael would have been looking forward to a warm reception in England where her published work had been well received. However, the move had tragic consequences. For a while Carmichael's literary work flourished – alongside the birth of four more children. Then Mullis appears to have deserted his young family. Living in desperation in the East End of London, at a time when no social welfare help was available, Carmichael sank into despair and poverty. She herself was admitted to a workhouse in Leyton in London. Two of her children died. The three remaining boys were placed in a workhouse in Northampton. Her poems in these dark times looked back to the old days in Gippsland when her life was full of promise.

Perhaps we can find room for one more poem to illustrate this. *To a Spray of Gippsland Wattle* was written during these bitter days in London. When a memorial was placed on her grave in after-years, some lines from this poem were included:

> *O! give me the little spray*
> *Of wattle, grown so far away!*
> *I'll hold it with a loving hand;*
> *Indeed thou cannot understand,*
> *All it will speak to me!*

> *If only a spray of wattle bloom,*
> *Looking at me amid the gloom*
> *Of city smoke and dust and glare.*
> *Drooping in uncongenial air —*
> *A spray, of wattle bloom,*

> *But every tiny bud and leaf*
> *Whispers to me, in tender grief.*

"Sweet soul that loved the forest so,
Wherein our myriad blossoms blow,
What has become of thee?"

Ah! little flower I loved of old,
Dear little downy heads of gold!
Truly, mine eyes are full of tears
As o'er the long dividing years,
The past comes back to me.

Surely thou knowest not from home—
Thy home and mine— I willing roam!
Ah! Could'st thou guess how fancy flies
To those bush shades and forest skies
Far from those city stones!

And yet, I thank thee, dearest flower,
Thou comest in a troubled hour
To whisper, 'mid the city's roar,
"Its noise is not for evermore;
The bush wilds wait for thee".

By the early twentieth century, English workhouses had lost their former image of depravity and hopelessness. The Leyton workhouse was a new building of two and three stories, well-designed and well-managed. Nevertheless the workhouses remained places of stern discipline and restriction of individual aspirations and freedoms. We can imagine the feelings of the bush child of Orbost, the young lioness of Australian literature, as she spent her days alone in a seething crowd, in a foreign land, amidst the wracking routines so far outside her control.

In the mid-winter of 1904, Carmichael, now aged thirty-seven, contracted pneumonia, and died on the ninth of February. She was buried without ceremony in the Wood Grange Park Cemetery nearby. Her death was briefly noticed in the Australian press. The *Australasian* noted:

[It was] from Orbost in Gippsland that she began sending us verses which from the first were marked by deep feeling and much power of poetical expression. ... She continued her contributions to our columns until recently. She wrote stories as well as verse, but her talent was most conspicuous in her poems which showed not only a complete command of rhythm, metre, and language, but thought and feeling that stamped her as something more than a writer of graceful verse.

For the next five or six years Carmichael's name disappeared from public view. The three boys languished under the care of guardians in the Northampton workhouse. Then came a sudden change for the better. The boys' situation was discovered by a fiercesome colonial woman, Miss C Hay Thomson, a Scottish-born undercover journalist. She used to undertake cloak and dagger assignments, such as disguising herself as a man to visit brothels and inns, then exposing their practices in her newspaper articles. In one infamous episode, she worked her way into the Kew Asylum as an attendant in order to report on practices there. Hay Thomson had met Carmichael through the Austral Club in Melbourne. On discovering the Carmichael boys' circumstances in England, she began a vigorous campaign to bring them home. She wrote to the Melbourne newspapers:

... after years of adversity, [Jennings Carmichael] died in circumstances of the direst poverty through no fault of hers. ... She deserved well of her country. Morally and intellectually she was an honour to it, and it is fitting that her country should repay the debt to the children she has left behind her, who are now, I am pained to have to say, the inmates of an English workhouse. Jennings Carmichael came to Melbourne from the Gippsland wilds.... During several years poems and sketches from her pen appeared almost every week in the columns of "The Australasian". At this time she was known in Melbourne circles as the "Gippsland poetess". ... Her three children (boys), whose ages are now 7, 10 and 13 years respectively are in the care of the Guardians of the poor in the Northampton Union Workhouse. The present whereabouts of the father, if he be alive, are unknown. ...

A few who remember Jennings Carmichael's early promise appreciate what her life must have been for [her last] seven or eight years and have become interested in her children's welfare now appeal to the Australian people to rescue these children for their own sake, no less than for their mother's. A sum of money has already been collected in Adelaide for this purpose. Could not a meeting of Miss Carmichael's friends and admirers be held and some attempt made to move in the direction proposed?

A great variety of fund-raising ventures now began, principally in Melbourne and Adelaide. The local campaign was launched by a large gathering in the Melbourne Town Hall attended by the social elite of the day. Dozens of fund-raising activities and entertainments were held, large and small. A Skating Party was held at the South Yarra rink, with accompanying entertainments. Money poured in from the larger country towns, all donations being published in the press. Fellow-Gippslander, singer Ada Crossley, was brought in to help spur subscriptions. May Vivienne, a well-known adventurer of the day, helped to whip up public support. Henry Lawson wrote a poem for his old friend, excoriating those who spend their wealth on luxuries, 'but not a penny that might save / the children of the Gippsland girl'. The Victorian government offered free passages home for the three boys. Donald McDonald, probably the most famous journalist in Australia at the time, lent a hand. Draining all the pathos he could from the situation, he wrote a long article in the *Argus* stressing Carmichael's bush upbringing, and concluding:

She wandered far from the old bush roads, from the home paths where still in the brush of the leaves are symphonies, and where some day to other singers the still, small voice may whisper the themes that are to live. And as a little human memorial to the poor singer who loved the land that we love, let us bring those three boys of hers back to her land and ours, and give them a chance, just for auld lang syne - for Sentiment's sake - for their mother's sake.

The boys – Geoffrey, Clive and Keith - did indeed arrive in Melbourne in October, 1910 and were settled into private homes in Geelong, Melbourne and Deniliquin, resuming their mother's maiden name of Carmichael. Geoffrey went to the family of the small disabled child his mother had nursed in Geelong twenty years earlier. When war broke out in 1914, Geoffrey enlisted and served overseas. Clive was on the point of enlisting when the war ended.

Meanwhile Carmichael's grave in London had been tended over the years by some women from St Cedd's Church in Canning Town. In 1927 the grave was 're-discovered'. A headstone was placed on her pauper's grave in the form of an open book. On one page were inscribed the words- 'A Wattle day Tribute, to the memory of Jennings Carmichael, an Australian poetess'. On the opposite page etched into the white marble, was a spray of her beloved golden wattle and a couplet from her poem, *To a Spray of Gippsland Wattle*:

> *Ah! little flower I had of old*
> *Dear little downy heads of gold!*

Some of her poems were recited as people stood around. Four years later, in January, 1931, another service was held at the graveside with local and Australian dignitaries present. Sprays of wattle blossom were placed on the grave.

Back in Victoria, a limited edition of her poems was published in 1910 with the help of a grant from the government of the day. During the Back-to-Orbost celebrations in 1937, a bronze panel depicting Carmichael was placed in the Shire Council chambers by a group of her admirers. It carried a fine bust of Carmichael and the words,

Grace Jennings Carmichael

Australian Poetess

1866 – 1904

Spent Her Childhood in this District

Carmichael's youngest son, Mr Keith Carmichael, now a businessman in Bendigo, was present and spoke at the gathering. At the same time a framed photograph of Carmichael was placed in the State School. Another similar memorial was placed in the City Library in Ballarat.

Let the *Argus* reviewer of Carmichael's works have the last word. He wrote, in 1922, in honour of this Gippsland girl, this one-time nurse, this 'sweet singer of Orbost':

The slender, youthful charm of the poetess, her earnestness, and the interest that her personality lent to the pictures she unfolded of the beauties of the Australian bushland, remain as a vivid memory long after the untimely mists of Fate have descended upon the white gowned figure, and the sweet voice sings no more.

GEOFFREY CORNISH

... who flew RAF bombers in the Second World War, helped to plan the Great Escape from Stalag Luft III, and practised medicine in Drouin and Warragul.

10th April, 1941, in the deep darkness of night. Flight-Lieutenant Geoffrey Cornish is at the controls of his Handley-Page Hampden light bomber over occupied Holland en route to the industrial centre of Essen when the plane is caught in a spider-web of searchlights, attacked by German fighters, and fatally disabled. Cornish guides the plane as far he is able to open country. The other three crew members are lost, but Cornish parachutes to safety.

Safety of a sort! Cornish lands in a farmyard and is tended by the sympathetic family, but the Gestapo quickly arrive and he is marched away to interrogation and imprisonment, ultimately, in the new prisoner-of-war camp, Stalag Luft III at Sagan, deep within German territory.

Geoffrey Cornish grew up in Perth. As a boy he was passionate about medicine and chemistry and found part-time employment in the University's Chemistry Department. But Cornish also carried a dream to learn to fly. As the Second World War approached, he joined the Royal Air Force, though still in Perth, his ultimate hope being to take a medical degree while serving in the Air Force. He was selected to join a batch of twenty-two young men to travel to Britain to undergo pilot training under the RAF's Empire Air Training Scheme. He left Fremantle on 21 August, 1939. The war broke out while he was at sea, on 1 September.

On landing, Cornish proceeded immediately to flight training at several air bases and on several types of aircraft. One of his one-to-one trainers was Wing-Commander Guy Gibson of Dambuster fame. Cornish credited his long period of safe sorties over enemy territory to Gibson's advice and instructions. Cornish received his wings on 10 April, 1940, the youngest Captain in Bomber Command. He was only nineteen. At that time, the average life expectancy of the men carrying out bombing raids over enemy territory was six weeks. Cornish had a charmed life until that fatal night exactly a year later when on his eighteenth sortie. His serving career seemed to be over. However, his work for King and Country was soon to take another form!

Cornish was first held in POW Camp Stalag Luft I at Barth in northern Germany, a camp for RAF officers, where Cornish was put to work in the kitchens. After the best part of a year, he was transferred with many others to a new camp built in the east of the country, close to the border with Poland – Stalag Luft III. (*Stalag Luft* is an abbreviation of *Stammlager Luft*, which means, simply, *Main Camp - Air*).

Stalag Luft III was commanded and staffed by members of the German Air Force, the *Luftwaffe*. Many of the guards were older men or those unfit for active service, perhaps recovering from wounds. The site was chosen mainly because the soft sandy soil made it unsuitable for tunnelling. After a year in the East Compound, in early April, 1943, Cornish was transferred to the newly-built North Compound nearby. North Compound was claimed to be escape-proof. The prisoners' huts were built half a metre off the ground to allow observation and inspection from below. Sensitive microphones were placed to pick up any signs of underground digging. Patrolling by guards was constant.

The camp eventually grew to twenty-four hectares in size and housed some 2,500 RAF officers, 7,500 US Air Force officers, and 900 officers from other Allied air forces, - a total of nearly 11,000 men. Prisoners in North Compound were housed in single-story huts, each 3.7 by 3.0 metres. There were eighteen men in each hut, sleeping in triple-decker bunks.

The prisoners in North Compound did their best to make it a home away from home. With the permission of the camp authorities and with a lot of help from the Red Cross, a library was established, university courses could be followed and exams taken, and a theatre built where slick productions were put on. There was a radio station broadcasting news and popular music. As well, two news sheets were produced, each appearing four times a week. YMCA representatives had access to the camp, and were able to supply sporting equipment, musical instruments and books, as well as material for the chaplains. As time went by, prisoners were able to take part in a variety of sports – volleyball, basketball, softball, boxing, football, and table tennis. As well, Geoffrey Cornish devised a fitness programme for prisoners – a course he developed years later in Victoria and Queensland as the Cornish Walking Program. This was a camp for officers, it is to be remembered, and by international treaty conditions were much better than in camps for other ranks.

Still, escape plans were constantly being made. The camp authorities fully expected this, and, on top of their constant surveillance, attempted to infiltrate spies into the camp under the guise of captured Allied servicemen. As a counter-measure, all newcomers were strictly interrogated by the Camp Escape Committee. Several infiltrators were detected in this way. Beyond this, where there was some doubt about the authenticity of a new arrival he was accompanied everywhere he went until his genuineness was finally established.

The first successful escape from Stalag Luft III took place in the older East Compound in October, 1943. Here, a 30-metre tunnel was dug, the entrance being concealed by a wooden vaulting horse set up close to the camp perimeter. Just three men were involved in the digging and the escape. After several months of tunnelling, the men successfully made their escape. All three made it back to Britain. This escape was later widely popularised through the book, *The Wooden Horse*, written by Eric Williams, one of the three escapees, and the subsequent film of the same name.

Now we come to the 'Great Escape' from North Compound, in which Geoffrey Cornish was a principal organiser. Even as the Wooden Horse escape was taking place, plans were being made for this much greater escape attempt. The brains behind it were those of a British prisoner, Squadron-Leader Roger Bushell. Around him was a tightly-knit and secretive committee which included Cornish. At the first meeting of the committee, Bushell spoke:

Everyone here in this room is living on borrowed time. By rights we should all be dead! The only reason that God allowed us this extra ration of life is so we can make life hell for the Hun ... In North Compound we are concentrating our efforts on completing and escaping through one master tunnel. No private-enterprise tunnels allowed. Three bloody deep, bloody long tunnels will be dug – Tom, Dick and Harry. One will succeed!

This was an escape attempt of massive proportions. Each escapee would be wearing civilian clothes and carrying forged papers. Many would have maps of the local area. All these things were produced surreptitiously within the camp.

The first tunnel – 'Tom' – began in Hut 123, beside the stove. Some time after tunnelling had begun it was discovered. Explosives were set and the tunnel destroyed. The second attempt – 'Dick' – began in Hut 122, the entrance hidden in a drain sump. The exit point was to be in a forested area beyond the camp boundary. However, while digging was in progress, this wooded area was cleared, and the tunnelling had to be abandoned. However the dig remained undiscovered and the tunnel was used to store soil from the next attempt and to hold supplies that would be needed by the escapees, such as maps, postage stamps, forged travel permits, compasses, and civilian clothing.

The third attempt – 'Harry' - was made from Hut 104, well away from the camp perimeter and thus not considered a likely escape point by the German authorities. The entrance was under the stove. The tunnel was very deep in order to avoid detection by the Germans' seismic equipment. From the entrance point, the tunnellers dropped vertically eight-and-a-half metres. From there the tunnel would extend horizontally for 102 metres to the woods beyond. Its course would take it directly under the administrative buildings of the camp authorities, including the Sick Bay and the Isolation Building, as well as under two barbed-wire installations. The tunnel itself was sixty centimetres square, although two larger staging posts were constructed along the way, where crudely-fashioned air pumps were installed. To prevent the sand from caving in, the tunnel was shored up with timbers scavenged from all over the camp, but particularly from the boards used as bases for the mattresses on the prisoners' beds.

Fellow-Australian, journalist Paul Brickhill, also an inmate of North Compound, graphically describes the tunnelling operation:

One lad, lying full length, hacked away at the sand, while his No 2, lying just behind, passed it back on the railway. Nearly every day, owing to the loose sand, there were dangerous falls at the face which held up work badly. The only warning would be a slight rustle and then No 1 digger would be buried under feet of suffocating sand, fallen from the roof. Our home-made lamps and airline would be smothered, and No 2, working fast, would have to grab his pal's feet in inky blackness, and haul him back out of danger.

Removal of the soil was done with metal scoops made from powdered milk cans. These cans were used also for making lamps in the dark tunnel. A piece of the metal would be made to hold the fuel (fat skimmed off the soup in the dining hut), the wicks being made from twisting fibres from camp clothing. The major problem was the disposal of the soil removed from the tunnel. This was achieved in a number of ways. False 'pockets' like long underpants were made, worn inside a pair of trousers. Where the sand could be safely dropped, it would be released and scattered. Sometimes sand was spread in the camp gardens, the sand being dug under as it was released. In cold weather, the men could conceal large amounts of soil under their great coats. In warm weather the sand could be carried in blankets used for sunbathing well away from the camp buildings. Another place for the dispersal of sand was in the hollow space under the back row of the picture theatre stalls. Extraordinarily, some of the German guards – some of them opposed to Nazism – helped the Escape Committee by providing railway timetables and maps so multiple copies could be forged. Others exchanged civilian clothes for the cigarettes, coffee, soap, and chocolate that was being sent to camp inmates in Red Cross parcels.

By March 1944 the tunnel was finished. Bushell and the Escape Committee would have preferred to wait until the warmer weather later in the year to activate the escape plan, but increased surveillance as a result of Gestapo pressure forced the decision to go while the cold and snow of winter still prevailed. 600 men had been involved in the escape preparations in some form or another, but it was decided that the number of escapees must be limited to 200. The choice of participants was extremely difficult. In the end, a priority system was used. The first 100 included seventy of the ones who had been most involved in the work and thirty others who had a record of previous escape attempts or who were proficient in German. The next batch of 100 was chosen by lot. They were considered to have a much reduced chance of success when on the run, and had less escape material such as maps allotted to them. As well, their lack of the German language would count severely against them.

Geoffrey Cornish played a key role in the escape preparations. Many of the planning meetings took place in his hut. He had learnt German whilst in camp and, through this, was part of the Bribery sub-committee. He was one of only seven men authorized to speak with the German guards. Underground, he was a tunnel shift organizer and worked himself in the tunnel. He was in charge of the photographing of documents for forgery purposes. Because of these contributions, he was allotted Place 8 in the first batch of escapees. However, he made a very difficult decision – almost certainly a life-saving decision as it turned out. Because of the medical knowledge and experience he had picked up, Cornish had been working as a medico and regularly accompanied the doctor – another prisoner - on his camp rounds. He felt that his work there was so important he gave up his escape bid and stayed behind to continue his work with sick prisoners. He thereby consigned himself to imprisonment and isolation for the duration of the war. 'Don't fence me in' remained a favourite song throughout Cornish's life!

After a week of waiting for a moonless night, the escape began after dark on the evening of Friday, 24 March. It was not without problems. The escape hatch was found to be frozen solid and it took an hour and a half to free it. Later, an air raid alarm caused the camp's lighting system to be shut down, bringing the tunnel also into total darkness. A collapse of sand meant a further delay. The first man through emerged at 10.30 pm. Unfortunately, something was amiss with the plans and it turned out that the exit was dangerously short of the dense forest cover. A guard tower was nearby. Tracks would be left in the snow between the escape hatch and the forest margin. To lessen the risk of being spotted, men were let through at the rate of one every six minutes instead of one every minute as had been the original plan. It was soon apparent that not everybody could get through before morning and the second batch of 100 was told that their hopes of escape were over and to return to their huts. In the event seventy-six men got through to the shelter of the woods. The seventy-seventh was spotted and the game was up. It was 4.55 am.

The escapees met huge obstacles. The temperature was below freezing. The snow was up to a metre and a half deep so the men had to stay on the roads. Those who had planned to catch trains found that the delays caused them to miss the night train services. Seventy-three of the seventy-six were rounded up. Only three got through, two of them reaching neutral Sweden and the other the British Consulate in Spain.

Hitler ordered the execution of the captured escapees, in clear contradiction to international law. In the end, fifty were shot, including the man who took Cornish's place in the escape, and the others returned to various prison camps, many of them back to Stalag Luft III. The murder of the fifty escapees was officially declared a war crime. Several Gestapo officers were executed following the War Crimes trials as a result. All his life Cornish carried with him the grief of the execution of his colleagues.

In the closing months of the war, as Russian forces approached from the east, the Stalag Luft III prisoners were marched and trucked in appalling mid-winter conditions 500 kilometres to Nuremberg. Cornish played a vital role in caring for the prisoners during this epic journey. American forces eventually liberated all prisoners on 3 May, 1945.

Cornish, however, immediately after liberation, volunteered to go to the ill-famed Dachau concentration camp to give medical assistance. This was a low point in his whole life experience. It was "the worst scene I can ever remember," he commented later. "I never want to see anything like it again. ... To see that look of incredible disbelief, relief, in somebody who was so ill that they virtually had nothing left, but they clung to life so fiercely you could see that they knew now that ... it was all worthwhile." Cornish spent the best part of the next year in England studying and working – and marrying his Welsh wife, Myra - before returning to Perth.

Cornish did the first year of medical studies in Perth, then transferred to Melbourne University, where one of his teachers was the famed Weary Dunlop. To supplement his income, Cornish turned his hand to other skills – working in Henry Bucks men's store and decorating wedding cakes! After graduation, the Cornishes moved to Bronte Park in Central Tasmania, where Geoffrey worked as medico to the bustling migrant population engaged in building the hydro-electric power stations nearby, and from there moved to Drouin, here in Gippsland, where Geoffrey was the partner of the celebrated local GP, Dr Edward Hamp. He remained in Drouin for four years, until 1956.

In Tasmania, Cornish had instituted the first regional blood bank collection system anywhere outside a capital city. One of the migrant workers he recruited to help him – Nicki Gottschalk - later trained as a pathologist and worked at Warragul and Bairnsdale

Hospitals. Now Cornish repeated this system at the Warragul Hospital. The Red Cross blood collection centre he established here was the first permanent one in regional Australia. Like many rural doctors of the time, Cornish was very inventive. To help his work in anaesthetics, then used by dentists and general practioners as well as in the hospital, he devised a portable machine that could be taken easily from place to place. He also developed a method of giving anaesthetics that enabled quicker and easier recovery. It was while in Drouin, too, that Cornish began to develop his walking system to help the recovery of cardiac patients, and for which he later became famous.

Geoffrey Cornish was a delightful man –wise, gentle, humble, though determined to the point of stubbornness, not at all concerned with personal recognition or financial gain. He and his family were fully involved in community life. In Drouin, Geoffrey joined Rotary, the beginning of over fifty years of Rotary membership in Victoria and later in Queensland. Geoffrey and Myra formed long-lasting friendships with Drouin people like the Colquhouns (the butcher), the Whiteheads (the baker), and the Drysdales (the dentist). The children rode horses and played with their friends. Adele, the older of the two Cornish girls, has spoken of the happy time she and her family spent in Drouin in the local history project, 'Voices of Drouin'.

Years later, after the Cornishes had moved to Frankston, they bought a property at Jindivick, north of Drouin, overlooking the

Tarago Reservoir. The hope was that the bracing air of the hill country would help Myra's chronic heart-lung weakness. Here they kept a menagerie of beasts and birds – donkeys to ride on, fowls to provide food for the table. However, the hoped-for benefits did not come for Myra, and the decision was made that Geoffrey and Myra would re-locate to the Gold Coast to seek relief there. Sadly, Myra died in Queensland. Geoffrey later re-married. He and his second wife, Alison, had many years together.

Through all this Geoffrey's work went on. He founded a new Rotary Club – the Surfers Sunrise Rotary Club, which, quite unlike other Rotary Clubs, meets at 7.00 am on Wednesday mornings at the Surf Life Saving Club. Nearby is the coastal walk named for him – the Cornish Walk. The Surfers Sunrise Rotary Club is renowned for its work in assembling wheelchairs and shipping them to places of great need throughout Asia and the Pacific, and even as far as Chernobyl.

On the Gold Coast, Cornish continued and perfected his walking system for cardio-vascular patients. Participants walk on a flat grassed area such as a football field around circular lines forming a wheel outwards from the centre. As each walker walks further from the centre they pass points (marked with colour-coded flags) so that the further they walk outwards the further and faster they need to go in the next stage. The programme for each person is devised and supervised by a health professional. Up to 125 patients of high, medium and low exercise capacities are able to walk together, so there are important social as well as medical benefits. Several thousands have taken part in the program over the years, many of them continuing the course long after being officially discharged from it. For his work in devising and introducing this system and for his general contribution to medicine, Geoffrey Cornish was awarded the Medal of the Order of Australia (OAM) in 1993.

Cornish returned three times to the scenes of his RAF exploits and his imprisonment. He was able to attend the twenty-fifth and fiftieth anniversaries of the Great Escape and, finally, the sixtieth anniversary in 2004. The latter was a particularly poignant occasion as he re-visited the site of Stalag Luft III, now completely destroyed and abandoned except for a few scattered items of debris. He met and presented flowers to the woman who, as a teenager, had seen to his wounds when he parachuted into her father's farm in 1941. He was also able to meet one of the Stalag Luft guards, Klemnitz, who had been responsible for the distribution of Red Cross parcels. Klemnitz had been acknowledged as being very fair and honest – and unbribable!

Geoffrey Cornish, OAM, died on 10 April, 2005, the same calendar date on which he graduated as a bomber pilot, was shot down over Holland, and later moved into North Compound in Stalag Luft III. He left a magnificent legacy in medical innovation and achievement. Add to that his outstanding career as a bomber pilot, followed by his heroic work in the prisoner-of-war camp. At home he was involved in compassionate humanitarian work, particularly with Rotary. Beside his public persona, Geoffrey Cornish was committed to his family and held in deep affection by them. He was a man driven by noble causes, engaging and optimistic. All his life he carried, mostly unspoken, a deep spirituality. His personal text came from the Gospel of St Luke: *Jesus grew in wisdom and stature and in favour with God and man.* He would apply this four-fold standard to himself and quietly recommend it to others. Towards the end of his life, he suggested that anything he had achieved in his life was due to two factors: 'faith and persistence'. Tara Brown, host of the TV program, '60 Minutes', one episode of which featured Geoffrey Cornish, described his life as the life of an adventure novel, yet more unbelievable. In the midst of it, the hero lived his life in total unconcern for the high regard that surrounded him on all sides.

ADA CROSSLEY

... who began her career in Tarraville and Yarram, rose to be the darling of the English concert hall, and sang frequently in private audience for Queen Victoria.

Some 150 years ago – in the 1870s – two small girls of much the same age were growing up in Gippsland, one in Orbost, the other in Tarraville.

Both were destined to achieve fame for themselves and their homeland, one in the written word, the other in music.

Both clung fiercely to their Australian identity, but both were to die in England, far from their birthplace, the one in poverty and shame, the other in the bright light of celebrity.

The tragic life of Grace Jennings Carmichael is revealed earlier in an earlier chapter. Now we turn to that other 'small girl' of Gippsland, whose life was so vastly different - the renowned contralto, Ada Crossley. For Ada, it was 'roses, roses, all the way'!

Ada was born in Tarraville in March, 1871. At that time Tarraville still had some of the trappings of commerce stemming from its position on the track from Port Albert to the goldfields of Walhalla and Omeo. Her father, Edward, carried on an ironmongery business. It was a man's world, although amongst the women, in particular, there was a lively cultural life, especially in music.

So it was that Ada's mother, Harriette, encouraged her to play the piano and to sing. We can imagine a crowded and busy family life, for it was a large family; Ada was the sixth surviving child. 'A regular rough bush youngster I was with my auburn pigtail', wrote Ada, later. Throughout her life, Ada liked to recall her girlhood in the bush. She wrote of her love for horses, of taking the reins of the four-in-hand Sale coach, of climbing trees, and killing snakes. On the other side of the coin, she also wrote, 'The piano was my world then, and I stuck to it most religiously'. It is said that she knew the rudiments of music before she could read. Ada began formal lessons at seven when she began piano tuition with a Mrs Hastings in Port Albert. When twelve she began playing the organ at several churches in Tarraville and Port Albert, making herself available when she was able to fit in with their service times. By this time she was making a name for herself as a singer. The local newspaper carried news of her early successes. In May, 1882, for instance, when eleven, she sang the popular American song, 'Listen to the Mocking Bird', at a charity concert in Port Albert, Mrs Hastings accompanying.

By the time she was in her mid-teens, Ada's family recognised that her voice should be given more professional training while it was still in the development stage. Accordingly, she went to live with a married sister in Berwick and began studies in both piano and voice in Melbourne. Her piano teacher was the renowned Alberto Zelman, whom Ada recalled as 'that shaggy little Italian, whose paper collars and bright squirrel-like eyes made a strange impression on me'. At the same time she began singing lessons with the equally-renowned soprano, Madame Fanny Simonsen, at her home in Carlisle Street, St Kilda. That meant a great deal of travelling from Berwick to Melbourne twice weekly. It was not long before Ada moved in to Mme Simonsen's home as a boarder. She remained there for two or three years, in which time Mme Simonsen 'posed my voice perfectly'. It was probably there that the English composer and conductor, Sir Frederic Cowen, who had come to the colony to present a grand musical festival in connection with the International Centennial Exhibition in Melbourne in 1888, heard Ada sing and was impressed by the beauty and purity of her voice.

Ada's first grand appearance was in a Philharmonic Concert at the Melbourne Town Hall in 1889. She was eighteen. Ada reported, 'I proudly forwarded the cheque to my father, who still more proudly returned it'. For the next five years, Ada was in constant demand to appear in oratorio and concerts in Melbourne and in Sydney. Amongst these many appearances, she was a principal performer at a series of Promenade Concerts at the Melbourne Cricket Ground. However, Ada warmed to her Sydney audiences more than to those in Melbourne.

In the opinion of good judges, stated the newspaper *Table Talk* in 1894, *Australia has not produced a better singer. With the Sydney people she is a great favourite, and she deserves to be, for she has a magnificent voice, whilst her physical attractions are more than ordinary.*

During these years Ada became the principal contralto for the Australian Church. The Australian Church had been founded in Melbourne by a breakaway radical Presbyterian minister, Charles Strong, in 1885. It attracted a wide range of followers, such as Alfred Deakin and Bernard O'Dowd, who, like Strong, were committed to social reform, but whose religious views were hardly conformist. We cannot be sure how far Ada was personally committed to the Church. However, beside her vocal contribution she was active in other ways, such as by opening bazaars and fetes for them.

Ada was determined to study and perform overseas. In 1894 a series of grand farewell concerts was arranged in Melbourne, Adelaide, and Sydney. They were riotously successful. By now, Ada was everybody's darling. Ada liked to conclude her performances by singing 'The Lost Chord', which together with 'Nearer my God to Thee' had become one of her signature songs. The papers reported her farewell Melbourne concert:

She was not allowed to leave the platform until after another outthrust of enthusiasm and a presentation made by Mr F.O. Mason, MLA for South Gippsland, the birthplace of Miss Crossley. Saturday was the lady's birthday, and Mr Mason handed her a wreath of rosebuds, etc., to which was attached a white satin ribbon bearing on it in gold letters, "with heartiest greetings of South Gippsland to Ada Crossley".

It was much the same story in Adelaide four days later. In Sydney, *my farewell was unusually demonstrative, and before the great Centennial Hall was opened for the performance wires were stretched all around from the balconies to the platform, along which flowers were whirled each time I appeared.*

Ada's welcome in London was assured by the success of Nellie Melba, the Melbourne soprano who had burst on to the English scene several years before. Melba personally welcomed Ada to London and advised her on her teachers. Ada's decision to study under Charles Santley displeased Melba, who had wanted her to go to Matthilde Marchesi in Paris. However, after some months with Santley, Ada complied and spent seven months with Marchesi.

Ada's London debut was at the Queens Hall in May, 1895, twelve months after her arrival. Queens Hall in Langham Place had been opened only two years earlier, with a capacity of 2,500 people. It was here that the 'Proms' began, and it became known as 'the musical centre of the Empire'. Performers of the like of Debussy, Ravel, Elgar, and Richard Strauss appeared here. Another opportunity occurred shortly afterwards when at short notice she filled in for the legendary singer, Clara Butt, at a concert in Manchester. The English public had discovered her. Critics wrote of her 'dignity, fine poise and style', of 'the luscious richness' of her voice, and its 'translucent purity of rock crystal'.

Ada often commented on the good luck that accompanied her, and the fortunate life she enjoyed. She recounted one such piece of good fortune from her earlier years:

At the last Leeds Festival I had the unique experience of being called from the audience by the late Sir Arthur Sullivan to sing the contralto music in "Elijah", for which another artiste had been set down; but who was absent from the hall owing to a misconception as to the time. I was engaged there for different other works, and, with Mrs. Andrew Black, was enjoying an "off" morning, sitting in the front row, ready for the full enjoyment of the performance. The call to the platform made the hall spin round before my eyes, but everybody was most kind, and my performance, absolutely at a moment's notice, was most cordially received.

Within a few years Ada had a repertoire of 500 sacred songs and ballads, ranging from Gluck and Handel to Richard Strauss, and had mastered German, French, Italian, Norwegian, Danish, and Russian. Several times Ada was invited to sing privately to Queen Victoria, as Melba had been before her. Ada liked to show one of the gifts the Queen had given her – a pendant featuring a gold star from which hung a knot in red enamel and diamonds.

In 1903, Crossley made her first international tour, visiting cities in USA and Canada, receiving rapturous notices. In New York, she recorded several songs, including her signature aria, Giordani's, 'Caro mio ben'. These were amongst the first recordings ever made; some of them can now be heard on the internet. After returning to

London, she set out in August for her first return to her homeland. First she visited Canada, and then crossed the Pacific to New Zealand. Her concerts were hugely attended and enthusiastically received. In New Zealand, the crowd took the horses out of the shafts of her carriage and pulled her themselves through the streets lined by cheering crowds.

Again, a huge reception awaited her in Sydney. Leaders of the nation gathered to welcome her. Over the next three months she sang in all six state capitals and also in many regional towns such as Goulburn, Wagga Wagga, Ballarat and Bendigo. With her concert associates, who included the brilliant young pianist, Percy Grainger, she filled the Sydney Town Hall five times. In Melbourne, 5,000 came to a reception at the Town Hall where she was welcomed by a shower of roses. 20,000 attended her concert in the Exhibition Building. Nor did she overlook her origins. On 28 October, 1903, her first Gippsland concert took place in Traralgon. The state government provided the state carriage for her journey. Then followed concerts at Leongatha and Yarram. On 18 December she arrived in Sale for a charity concert in the Victoria Hall to raise money for the Sale Hospital. Three days later, the touring party moved on to the Theatre Royal at Bairnsdale. We might dwell on the Sale visit, as reported in the Maffra Spectator, to give the flavour of Crossley's Gippsland tour. Tickets for this concert were more costly than for Melbourne or Sydney – ten shillings for reserved seats, five shillings for unreserved, and two and sixpence 'down the back':

The following programme has been arranged in connection with Miss Ada Crossley's visit to Sale: The artiste who will arrive by the morning train on Tuesday will be met at the station by the Mayor and Mayoress, with the Councillors and the Town Clerk and Mrs Holt. Then drive to the Hospital, where Miss Crossley will be received by the President (Mr D. Nicolson). From there Miss Crossley will be driven to the Latrobe Bridge, returning by one of the Sale steamboats, which has been placed at the Mayor's service by the directors of the company. From the boat Miss Crossley will be driven to her hotel; and in the afternoon the Mayor and Mayoress will have an "At Home" in the Victoria Hall to which a large number of guests have been invited to meet Miss Crossley.

On the return voyage to England (via further concert triumphs in South Africa), Ada met on board a young Adelaide doctor, Francis Muecke. Romance followed and they were married at All Soul's, Marylebone, in April, 2005. The wedding was copiously reported in the Australian press:

The sacred building was profusely decorated with Lent lilies, white lilac, azalias, and palms ... the choir in their white surplices sang, 'The Voice that Breathed o'er Eden'. ... The bridal gown was of exquisite white chiffon made with a coat effect, and long ends of Spanish lace, held in with a ceinture of soft white satin, finished with paste buttons and a yoke lightly embroidered in silver, the skirt being arranged at the foot with a trimming of the same lace and satin. A court veil of white tulle fell from a coronet of orange-blossom, a sprig of the same flower being tucked into the bodice. At the conclusion of the service, a choir of women friends of the bride sang, 'O Perfect Love'.

It was a very happy marriage, though there were no children. Dr Muecke became a leading London throat specialist. The couple first lived in a cottage in St John's Wood, then in a fine home in Cavendish Square. In the First World War, Dr Muecke served on the Western Front, at one stage being in charge of the large field hospital at Rouen where many Australian troops were treated.

Following her triumphant overseas tour, Crossley's career resumed unabated. However, in 1908-09 she made an all-state return tour of Australia and New Zealand, equally as successful as the one five years earlier. Like the first, this second tour was under the auspices of JC Williamson's, and again featured Percy Grainger as an associate performer. It was something of a marathon, however, lasting eight months and covering 133 performances. The Gippsland leg of the tour was similar to the previous visit – concerts in Yarram, Leongatha, Sale, Bairnsdale, and Traralgon. This left the citizens of Warragul seething:

Why the central town of Warragul is over looked by the management for the great singer is inexplicable, and certainly very disappointing. ... We are convinced that if the illustrious singer had visited this centre of a large extensive district, the Warragul public hall, which is capable of accommodating nearly 1000 people, would scarcely have afforded seating room for the enthusiastic admirers of Gippsland's favourite and charming songstress.

During the First World War Crossley gave many charity performances to raise funds for the war effort and entertained many Australian soldiers in her London home. As well, she was frequently asked to sing at grand occasions of state. One of these was at the funeral of King Edward VII. Another was at the ceremonial laying of the foundation stone of Australia House in The Strand. Another was at the Memorial Concert held in London after the sinking of the Titanic. Crossley's name has always been associated with the Titanic, although the connection is rather convoluted. One of Crossley's favourite concert items was the hymn, 'Nearer my God to Thee'. She sang it, not to the tune familiar to many people now, but to another arrangement, 'Autumn'. After the Titanic hit the iceberg in 1912 and was sinking, the eight-piece ship's orchestra played that tune, 'Nearer my God to Thee', until the last moment. The incident quickly became part of the folk-lore associated with the tragedy.

Some time later, the British Orchestral Association mounted a memorial concert for those Titanic musicians at London's Royal Albert Hall. It featured a 500-strong orchestra composed of members of London's seven main orchestras—the Philharmonic, the Queen's Hall, the London Symphony, the New Symphony, the Beecham Symphony, the Royal Opera, and the London Opera

House. The conductors included Thomas Beecham, Henry Wood, and Edward Elgar. The feature artist was Ada Crossley, who sang the hymn, no doubt to the intense emotion of everyone present.

After the War, Crossley began to scale down her appearances, and in December, 1919, announced her retirement. She was then forty-eight years old. She continued to entertain younger performers in her home, especially Australians, and encouraged them in their careers. She regularly held Sunday afternoon tea parties for younger visiting Australians. One of those she supported was the South Australian Clara Serena, another contralto, who, as her mentor, Ada Crossley, had done before her, achieved huge success in England and elsewhere.

Ada's later years were marked by gracious outreach to others. Many speak of her 'domesticated and unassuming ways and of the entire absence of affectation'. Her health declined after an operation in 1919 and for a time she lost interest in singing. As her health improved, however, she began to recover her will to sing. In February, 1923, she stepped out of her retirement to sing in the Wigmore Hall with her younger friend, Clara Serena. A friend described her at that time:

Her voice is still very beautiful. And her appearance is wonderful. She does not look a day more than 40. Her figure is beautifully slim and graceful, and there is scarcely a line on her face. She is much handsomer than she was as a girl.

In October, 1929, Ada died after suffering a stroke. The funeral was at All Soul's, Marylebone, where she had been married. The Australian papers carried the news of her death and funeral in great detail:

ADA CROSSLEY is dead. In the little church of All Souls', which is so close it can almost touch hands with the Queen's Hall, where she made her first great triumph in London, Ada Crossley was borne on October 20, amidst a wealth of flowers.

The little church was gay for the harvest festival, with bunches of corn, and the rich reds and golds of autumn flowers. ... The mourning crowd wept quietly as she was carried by. If ever a woman was loved by her fellow artists, it was Ada Crossley. Though she had given up her public career as a singer, she poured out her love of music in generous assistance to the young, the struggling, the unknown. How many singers to-day can thank Ada Crossley for their first help and encouragement, particularly the young Australians. ... To-day a great wreath of yellow wattle lay upon the coffin, and with it an Australian flag. In that mourning crowd were many singers, distinguished ones and obscure, and people - just people who had loved her.... The service was simple. A lovely tenor voice sang. "O Rest in the Lord" and voices that can fill many a concert hall joined in "Nearer, My God, to Thee". Dr. Muecke, Ada Crossley's husband, with all the household staff, followed the coffin as the poignant funeral march of Chopin died away.

It is difficult to assess Ada Crossley's place in the musical Pantheon. The style of singers, especially of contraltos, has changed over the years. To the modern ear, Crossley often sounds heavy – one modern critic used the word, 'hooty' – but it also needs to be considered that we hear her voice only through the medium of crackling old shellac resin discs. Certainly she thrilled her listeners. Crossley was known best for her popular arias and sacred songs like 'Caro mio ben' and 'Nearer my God to Thee'. More classically inclined critics rated her renderings of the Agnus Dei from Bach's B minor Mass and the solo contralto part in Brahms' Rhapsody as amongst her greatest achievements.

A large mural depicting Ada Crossley was painted on the Mechanics Institute Hall in Yarram in 2020. It shows Ada with various symbols of her magnificent career around her. It is a fitting tribute in the very place where she sang many years ago both at the beginning of her career and in her days of triumph.

Earlier, in December, 2011, a monument to Crossley was placed at the BHP Esso Billiton Centre in Sale. Designed by the celebrated local designer, Annemieke Mien, it consists of a bronze-coloured plaque, with the regal figure of Crossley standing proudly in a setting of Australian flowers. A large treble clef and some musical text are beside the figure, while in the distance is one of the great music halls in which she performed. The text beneath reads:

Ada Crossley 1871-1929.

Contralto with special gift for oratorio.

Became an international celebrity, and gave several command performances for Queen Victoria.

Born in Tarraville, Gippsland, she grew up in the Yarram District.

Returned to Gippsland on triumphant concert tour including concert in Victoria Hall, Sale, in 1903.

We might conclude this account of the life of Ada Crossley where we began – by thinking of her in relation to her Gippsland contemporary, Grace Jennings Carmichael. In 1904, as Grace lay dying in her London workhouse, Ada was returning from her thrilling first Australian tour to her home in St John's Wood. They were within a Gippsland coo-ee of each other. How wonderful if Grace had been able to reach out to Ada! How sad that Ada did not know of Grace's plight!

JEAN GALBRAITH

... who lived quietly in her garden cottage in Tyers for ninety years, yet became celebrated here and abroad as a botanist and superb writer on the beauties of nature.

In 1939 Jean Galbraith wrote of the garden around her cottage, 'Dunedin', in Tyers:

It is not a model garden with terraces and wide peaceful lawns; rarely, alas, is it even orderly for Father, Mother and I are the only gardeners, except when the tall brothers come home for holidays. ... It is above all a place of flowers and trees, of roses climbing over arches. ... There are Delphiniums in it, and tall Foxgloves, gay common Marigolds and Poppies and Daisies; varied foliages, green against grey, grey against brown and red; bulbs that flower in the grass and wattles that smile at each other on winter days, fruit trees and blossom trees and many clustered vines.

In these few words we see the lightness of her touch, her sense of humour, and her respect for the things of nature. Jean honoured her flowers by always giving them a capital letter!

There was nothing but charity in her soul. As Civil War in Spain raged and the clouds of World War gathered in that same year, her heart was set on peace. If we all were to love the beauty of nature, she believed, how could we ever go to war?

... even in tortured Spain there are trees and flowers blossoming and around innumerable homes in Germany and Italy, as in England, flowers are tended and loved by peaceful-hearted folk who want nothing but to live quietly and to grow their flowers.

Jean Galbraith was born in January, 1906. She came of Scottish stock, and her forebears came to Gippsland from Beechworth, driving their dray over the mountains to their selection on the unpromising land rising over the Latrobe River valley. Jean was a delicate child and missed a lot of school. "Nobody ever taught me to write," she says. Yet when she was eleven she won second prize in a state-wide essay competition for schoolchildren run by the Gould League. The topic was 'Birds in Spring-time'. The same year she won first prize in an essay competition run by 'Cinderella' in the Melbourne newspaper supplement, the *Leader*. When the inspector came to the Tyers school in March, 1921, to examine the children for their Merit Certificate, Jean was amongst the seven who passed.

Jean first made her mark as an inveterate and impulsive letter-writer, first to family members and later to newspapers and scientific journals. Her cheerful and enquiring nature comes through in every line. Thus, when she was eleven, to her father in hospital:

Dear Daddy, I had a time of great excitement this week, and what with Flower Day and a trip to Traralgon and a walk on Sunday there has been a great deal of running about. On Flower Day I got up at half past five. I made thirty bouquets and altogether we got twelve pounds five shillings. Coming home we had three adventures. We saw a blue wren at the river and stopped to look at a firetail's nest, and Uncle Harry got an egg from it to take home to Arthur. As we were passing Moe we saw three very curious birds ...

A little later, still a schoolgirl, she began to make systematic notes of her nature observations. She carried her notebooks with her on her excursions into the bush and illustrated her notes with her hand drawings. Meredith Fletcher has included some of these in her *Jean Galbraith: Writer in a Valley*:

Aug 20 (1919) Found Everlastings and bacon and eggs. Golden wattle in full beautiful bloom. One tree seems to have bright red stems and is very beautiful. I wonder if it is a seperate [sic] species.

August 21. Found a green orchid quite new to me. We call it the brown throat because each blossom is like a wide opened mouth with brown throat and tongue. The flowers are small and there are about a dozen on each stem.

Jean was born into a family with strong Christian convictions. The Galbraiths were members of the Christadelphian church, which differs from the mainstream denominations chiefly in not accepting the doctrine of the Trinity. Jean's grandfather was wont to enter into religious dispute with others, writing long and fervent expositions of 'the truth' in the letters columns of the *Traralgon Record* and further afield. Jean lived her faith with a light and gentle touch. As the *Sydney Morning Herald* wrote in its obituary for Jean, *She was deeply religious and her natural warmth found its focus in loving friendship with those sharing common interests. In her case, this meant with women and men who shared her passionate involvement with the natural world.*

By the time she was nineteen Jean was emerging as an authoritative figure in the world of native plants. It was wildflowers that were to become her greatest love and her greatest field of expertise. Still in her teens, she would travel down from Traralgon on the train to the wildflower displays in the Melbourne Town Hall or the St Kilda Town Hall. There she met HB Williamson. Like Jean, Williamson began as an amateur collector from country Victoria and by now had become a leading authority on local flora. He encouraged Jean to send flowers to him for identification and classification. Within two years, Jean had sent 426 different plant species, all individually identified. We can imagine the voluminous correspondence that took place between them.

Becoming known in Melbourne, Jean met the editor of the monthly journal, the *Garden Lover*, Ralph Boardman, which led to her adopting the pen-name, 'Correa' and beginning a series of articles for that magazine, which she kept up for the next fifty years. She wrote beautifully – clearly, unpretentiously, and always redolent with the atmosphere of the bush. Here are her instructions for collecting sweet bursaria. (It should be noted that it was not until 1931 that our native wildflowers were protected by legislation):

Use a sharp trowel to lift the young seedlings growing under the older plants; wrap them firmly in moss or grass and take them home to place in pots. A year later, plant them in the garden. Put them in a corner where they have room to stretch their thorny arms ... and they will give you the joy of blossom, and the scent of summer riversides.

Jean was fortunate to have several sympathetic mentors as her expertise developed. HB Williamson and Ralph Boardman were the first. Donald Macdonald and Charles Barrett also helped Jean enormously. Then there was John Inglis Lothian. Lothian was a Melbourne family man of some substance. Formerly in the publishing business, he developed a keen interest in native flora and fauna. After he wrote to Jean praising one of her articles, a close friendship developed between them, entirely by correspondence for many years. In all their letters she was 'Correa', and he 'Grandfather'. They eventually met by arrangement at a wildflower show in the City. Clearly a tender relationship existed between them, although when Jean was twenty-one, Lothian was seventy.

Jean never married. However, another close friendship was soon to come. Walter Thornby was a TB patient in a Melbourne hospital. In her articles, Jean always referred to him as 'the Artist'. The friendship began when Jean and her father sent, via the cream truck and onward by train, carefully prepared boxes of flowers to the Austin Hospital where Walter was a patient. The flowers were shared joyfully around Walter's ward. Letters were exchanged and then, one great day, Walter came to visit … and, later, to stay. Jean's father built him a bungalow to sleep in and Walter did what he could around the garden. Jean wrote of his gentle presence among the family:

… The garden welcomed him; the shade under the wide boughs of the oak became his livingroom, … and there Mother and I took our needlework; there we made glowing plans for the garden, planted seeds and potted plants and found more laughter than our quiet garden had known for years. … He planned our rock garden pond and designed the sundial. The wooden birds that protected the buds on our bluebell tree were his carving; so were the polished wooden windmills whose spinning delighted the children. Every rose knew his touch …

One morning he died there in his bungalow. Jean wrote to 'Grandfather':

He died quietly just after he woke in the morning. There is a break and a blank in our home life, but it is less the blank of death than of a friend gone to a far country to rest and grow strong. I kept his fountain pen and a prayer book. … And so another page of life closes for me.

By the mid-1930s, while Jean was still in her 'twenties, she was widely known as a leading figure in the world of native flora and fauna. Her articles and photos were now being published in American nature journals, bringing in precious funds. The first letters she received from the United States publishers were addressed to 'Mr Galbraith' – a reminder that Jean was breaking barriers in a man's world. At the other extreme, Jean was being sought after locally. In 1935, for instance, she travelled to the Bulga Park in the Strzeleckis at the invitation of the Yarram Progress and Tourist Association. (Someone must have driven her for Jean never owned a car!) There she named trees and plants in the Bulga Park and the Tarra Valley Park (as they were then) so name plates could be fixed to them for the benefit of tourists and students. While there she demonstrated her closeness to the ways of nature. The Shire Engineer told the story at the next meeting of the Progress and Tourist Association:

Miss Galbraith had a wonderful way of attracting birds. Hearing the note of a bird, she asked, "Would you like to see that yellow-breasted one?" Whereupon, by imitating the cry of a chick bird in distress, she had all the birds in the place around her.

Jean's letters and articles were now appearing monthly in the *Garden Lover* and the *Victorian Naturalist*, as well as in the *Age*, the *Argus*, and the *Australasian*. Many of her *Garden Lover* articles consisted of homely descriptions of her own garden at Tyers and how she and others in the family built it bit by bit over the years.

With the encouragement of many others, particularly John Lothian, she now decided to publish a book simply telling the story of the garden, drawing on these published articles as a basis for the work.

The book came out in 1939 with the title, *Garden in a Valley*. Priced then at 2/6, it can now be bought, second-hand, on eBay for $40.00! Most would regard the book as priceless. There is no preaching about how things should be done. There is no claim to superior knowledge. There is no false sentimentality. It tells the simple story of how a family – Jean and her mother and father, assisted occasionally by brothers and cousins, nephews, nieces and friends - turned a raw piece of Gippsland hillside into a place of warmth and beauty. Paths are made, drains dug, wild flowers transplanted, rock gardens established, vegetables introduced, a water fountain constructed, and flowering shrubs and trees placed to best advantage. All over Australia people were being brought to see their own place through different eyes, imagining and applying Jean's down-to-earth love of her land to their own situation. The book was handsomely re-printed in 1985.

Garden in a Valley was published just as war was breaking out in Europe, soon to engulf Australia as well. Jean felt the oncoming tragedy deeply. Her own life at that time was not free from personal sadness. Her brother, Laurie, now married to Linette and lecturing in Civil Engineering at Melbourne University, was trapped in a blizzard while hiking on Mount Hotham with a friend. He had a heart attack and died before rescuers could reach him. On hearing the news she wrote to John Lothian in grief, but also from the depths of her faith:

I am going to Linette at once ... You know all our hope and joy (ours and Laurie's and Linette's also) is in the thought of the return of the Lord Jesus ... and we feel that the parting may not be for long. Do not be too sad for us: the world is still beautiful.

Within a few months her friend and mentor, John Inglis Lothian was dead also.

While *Garden in a Valley* might inspire others in a general sense, Jean was also busy in more direct and practical ways. In 1950 her field guide, *Wildflowers of Victoria* appeared, a boon to amateur nature lovers. It could easily be taken into the bush to help with identification. Meredith Fletcher refers to it as a 'glove-box bible'. She goes on, 'Still people say when they go for a drive in the bush, "Will we take Jean Galbraith?"'

Twenty years later Jean extended her range by publishing *Collins Field Guide to the Wild Flowers of south-east Australia.* This was a work of biblical proportions – 512 pages with copious illustrations. The work firmly established Jean in the top rung of authority in the field of native Australian plants.

Although she never married and lived by herself after the death of her parents, Jean was never alone. She rejoiced in the company of her wide family and her many friends. She once made an intrepid journey with women friends in a very unreliable vehicle to Sydney, travelling over the mountains on the outward journey and back around the coast. Then a dream was realised for her when she scraped together enough money to take a trip to the Grampians to see the wildflowers there at first hand. She found delight wherever she went.

Meanwhile, Jean was constantly working with others in her field. One such connection was with the noted botanical artist, Betty Conabere. The two of them spent a week at Wilsons Promontory in search of wildflowers in 1970. Jean told how she would spend the afternoons finding flowers, while Betty would spend the whole day painting them. A little later, Betty came to stay with Jean at Tyers. Again, Jean would go out to find the flowers for Betty to paint. Another collaborator was Edna Walling, the pre-eminent landscape gardener of the time. The two carried on a correspondence over many years before they met. No doubt under some influence from Jean, Walling moved more and more towards the use of native plants in her gardens. Walling's niece, Barbara Barnes, has written of the work done by the two women together:

Jean Galbraith had a working relationship with Aunt. Jean Galbraith was a botanist and she helped Aunt enormously with identifying plants. They went for trips together and shared a love of wild flowers and searching for wild flowers. Jean would identify them and Aunt would photograph them. They kept up a correspondence and that was definitely a professional correspondence as well as one of affection and companionship....

Jean was immensely helpful when Aunt was trying to get a book published which was to do with a trip they had shared. Jean identified all the photographs that Aunt took. .... Jean wrote reams and reams of very professional letters identifying plants and helping and doing the best she could.

The book was eventually published, posthumously for both women, under the title, *On the Trail of Australian Wildflowers*.

As the years went by, Jean was drawn increasingly to environmental concerns. She did not have to look far for evidence of the degradation of the landscape. The Tyers River which ran 'almost at her doorstep' had suffered hugely from development along its reach. In one of her articles for the *Australian Garden Lover*, in July, 1935, she poured out her grief at the state of the river. Farming in the upper reaches and land clearing along the whole length of the stream had caused great damage. Jean used the river to speak the words for her:

'Don't you know that with unclothed banks I must work my own destruction, washing away, scouring out?' the river asked. Its warning was ignored. A quick succession of floods scoured the banks, destroyed fences and bridges and inundated houses. The river was choked with debris. ... For beauty there was desolation, for fruitfulness barren sand, for riches poverty. The water catchments were denuded to make men rich, the lowland banks were cleared for little gain, and the result filled the valley with fear.

The next year, 1936, Jean donated a piece of her land to be run as a wildflower sanctuary by the Native Plants Preservation Society of Victoria. If you go to Tyers today you can find and enjoy the walking track in the Jean Galbraith Reserve. "0.19 kilometres; 3 minutes; very easy", the advertising says. It adds, for the benefit of the uninitiated, "Any fan of botany will have heard of Jean Galbraith. Visit her home turf where she lived for over 90 years. This flora reserve is a tribute to her work and a lovely place to picnic".

More than twenty years later Jean could still find no joy in the local situation. Responding in the *Argus* in July, 1949, to a letter about the preservation of native flowers, she wrote:

...If we are to preserve small local sanctuaries as suggested, we must act quickly. Traralgon and Morwell have no unspoiled native bush close to the towns (if one excepts the railway reserves, which are the last strongholds of the smaller flowers). Small towns like Herne's Oak which, even four or five years ago were set in gardens of flowers, have now only remnants struggling to exist. Even near the township where I live, six miles from a railway or main highway, there is not one place where wildflowers grow in profusion. If we act now, protecting small areas - river banks, angles, or strips between roads and bits of wasteland-from rabbits and noxious weeds, they will re-generate themselves, for there are still seeds in the ground.

Jean Galbraith wrote other books. Apart from those mentioned above, the list includes *Fruit*, 1966, *Wildflower Diary* (with Winifred Waddell), 1976, *A Gardener's Year*, 1987, and *A Garden Lover's Journal*, 1989.

There are three nature books for children: *Grandma Honeypot*, 1963, *From Flower* to *Fruit* (with Moira Pye), 1965, and *The Wonderful Butterfly*, 1968.

Doongalla Restored, 1991, drawn from Jean's journal articles of half a century earlier, is the imaginative account of a couple restoring an old garden in the Dandenongs.

Kindred Spirits, 1999, consists of the botanical correspondence between Jean and Anne Latreille.

Besides these prose works, Jean published, *Poems for Peter*. She was also a frequent contributor to the New South Wales *School Magazine*, and wrote for ABC radio. She had a monthly page in the *Educational Magazine* on the subject of the preservation of native plants. Finally, Jean wrote the words for several hymns.

In 1970 Jean was awarded the Australian Natural History medallion by the Field Naturalists Club of Victoria. She stands alongside such eminent recipients as AH Chisholm, David Fleay, Charles Mountford, Crosbie Morrison, Thistle Stead, Vincent Serventy, and fellow-Gippslander, Tarlton Rayment.

Three species of plants have been named in her honour – *Prostanthera galbraithiae*, *Boronia galbraithiae*, and *Dampiera galbraithiana* The *Prostanthera* – Wellington mint bush- was discovered by Jean in the Holey Plains State Park, near Rosedale. She long advocated for its protection. Jean's Wellington mint bush at Holey Plains is now fenced off for protection and, despite the recent fires there, is doing well. It adorns the cover of this book.

Jean Galbraith's name is held in honour far beyond the little cottage in Tyers where she spent virtually the whole of her life. She is universally loved and respected. There is much more to that than her botanical expertise. It has to do with the purity of her motivation, the sincerity of her dealings with others, and way she saw the world as a whole, brought togetherin imagination and spirituality, and finally by the lyrical beauty of her writing. That is the point on which to finish. Who can not be moved by such a passage as this, from the very first page of her *Garden in a Valley*, as she recalls the days of her youth?

Years and years of nights, it might have been, we lay in the warm dusk and smelled the fragrance of white jessamine starlike round the open window, and heard the friendly "plomp" of frogs in the pool under the wide black wattle trees. Years and years of mornings we traced the words of "The Lord is my Shepherd" on the long scroll-like picture on the wall, heard the clear note of the grey thrush and hastened out to the veranda with crumbs, saw the garden brimming with roses, the slopes of blossoming orchard on every side, our own gardens, each with its special treasures. Years and years, stretching back to dim forgetfulness, we saw the lamplight across the dusk, and lazily traced the pattern of lilies on the wall, and were sung to sleep, dreamy and warm and as safe as nestling birds.

SIR KEITH HANCOCK

... a rouseabout boy from Bairnsdale who went on to grace the great universities of the world and has been called Australia's greatest historian.

Keith Hancock's father was a pioneering clergyman in Bairnsdale and the boy lived his whole life in awe and admiration of his father. In his autobiographical *Country and Calling*, Hancock jnr speaks lovingly of his father and his down-to-earth way of dealing with the floating bush population of Bairnsdale in the first years of the twentieth century. He tells this story of his father:

There were the poor parishioners he helped. On top of all these was the brazen and boozy fraternity of tramps. Did they, as we believed, have a secret mark on our gate post? Or did they hand on from one to the other the news that the Parson in Bairnsdale was easy game? I doubt whether a single one of them ever passed through our town without coming to Father with a hard luck story. He seldom swallowed the story but always heard it out as a prelude to his own game, which he opened by sniffing the liquor scented air.

'You've been drinking!'

'Strike me pink Mister, I ain't touched a drop the whole blooming day!'

'Let me feel your pulse.' (A pause) 'Why, you must have had a dozen drinks!'

'Mister, I ain't had more than three and that's God's truth!'

Maybe in the end a compromise would be reached at four or five drinks, and Father, looking very pleased with himself, would call out to Mother to get a meal ready for a hungry man.

Hancock reminisces lovingly about his days boating, swimming, fishing, and fighting in and alongside the Mitchell River which flowed not far from the Parsonage front door. He tells, too, of the time he and his younger friend, Ronnie Dahlsen, were at the river when Ronnie fell into deep water. Hancock pulled him out and saved Ronnie's life. Ronnie promised to give him all the money in his money box as a reward (*'Drat him! He never did!'*), but the greater reward was that the Royal Humane Society awarded him a bronze medal for bravery.

The family moved to Melbourne in 1908 when Keith was ten, but Hancock was to look back in fond remembrance of Bairnsdale all his life. He maintained one personal connection with Gippsland, however. His sister, Dora, married Percy Dicker, the heroic padre at Yallourn in the days when Yallourn was a tent town and the miners were a rough and tough gaggle of men from all over the world.

In Melbourne, Hancock exchanged the rough and tumble of the Mitchell River for the world of books. He went through Melbourne

Grammar and then Trinity College at Melbourne University with the aid of scholarships. On graduating, he was appointed as Assistant Lecturer in History at the University of Western Australia, this beginning a brilliant trail of appointments in both Australia and England. From Perth, to his amazement, for he was not a sportsman, he won a Rhodes Scholarship, which allowed him to proceed with a degree in Modern History at Balliol College, Oxford. These were heady days, but Hancock never forgot his humble beginnings and his Gippsland origins. He longed to once again 'make my way with two or three friends along the ridges and gullies [of Gippsland] to habitations fifty or more miles apart from each other', but for the moment the call of scholarship and career was too strong. He remained in England.

After completing his degree at Balliol, Hancock was elected to a fellowship at All Souls, Oxford, the first Australian ever to be so awarded. Hancock's biographer, Jim Davidson, in *Keith Hancock: the Three Cornered Hat,* has commented, 'All Souls gradually became an English home, one to which he would return periodically for the rest of his life'. Hancock jested of his appointment, recalling the story of the poor man and his wife who had two sons 'of whom one ran away to sea and the other became a Fellow of All Souls and was never heard of again'. He relished the 'pomp and circumstance' of his life there, but secretly hankered after an invitation to join the Husteron Proteron Club which ate its dinners backwards, from the cigars and coffee, through the raisins and port, the pudding, joint and fish, the claret and hock, to the final course of soup and sherry!

Meanwhile, Hancock had fallen in love with Italy. He researched and published a book on the *Risorgimento*, the nineteenth-century movement that led to the driving out of foreign overlords and the unification of the Italian states to form a united Kingdom of Italy. In all his research work, Hancock held to one primary consideration – the need to 'walk the ground' and not merely rely on records and published accounts of the subject under study. He followed this principle with his *Risorgimento*, although this approach was never more evident than in his *Discovering Monaro*, written many years later, after Hancock's retirement from the Australian National University in Canberra.

While at Oxford, Hancock married Theaden (Thea) Brocklebank, whom Keith had met when they were undergraduates in Melbourne. Thea had gone on to teach at Frensham in New South Wales. She was a cultivated woman and later became an outstanding talks producer for the BBC, but it was not a happy marriage. Sadly, Thea was unable to have children following a hysterectomy.

The Hancocks returned to Australia in 1926 when Keith took up the chair of Modern History at Adelaide University. He was twenty-eight years old, the youngest professor in the British Commonwealth. The Hancocks remained in Adelaide for seven years. Here Hancock wrote his small volume, *Australia*. This is a remarkable book, written when Hancock was just thirty-two, and covering the whole sweep of settlement in its 65,000 words. Perhaps it is more an extended essay than a historical work. However it has had a profound effect on later interpretation of our history. One reviewer has commented that the book has gained something of a cult status, 'especially among those who are opposed to government intervention in the economy'. Another wrote: 'In 1930 this was the most professional and profound single volume about the country, and remains so'. Another has put it:

This was history written in and for the present, drawing big pictures, exposing the central issues of Australian society, trying not in the tired modern phrase to be relevant but in a much more vital way to be effective.

I still have the battered copy I used in classrooms half a century ago.

From Adelaide, Hancock once more heard the call from England, and accepted an appointment as Professor of History at Birmingham University. His principal and outstanding achievement there was his monumental two-volume *Survey of British Commonwealth Affairs*. Hancock is shown as a staunch supporter of the good done over the years by British imperialism. The economist, Noel Butlin, comments:

His massive works on British Commonwealth affairs transformed the way in which not only studies but the actuality of Empire and Commonwealth were perceived.

In 1939 war broke out between Britain and Germany. Hancock was still in Birmingham and immediately dug up a plot of land to produce vegetables, then enlisted in the Home Guard. In his *Country and Calling*, Hancock recalls those days:

I dug spade for spade alongside my friends in our immense allotment and when the enemy dropped a bomb at the edge of it I planted daffodils in the disfigured ground beside our vegetables. I gave up many afternoons for the Home Guard and as Sergeant of Section V11 of the University Battalion took responsibility one night in every week, and sometimes oftener, for manning our observation post on the top of the great tower.

There was other important wartime work to be done, however – work more suited to Hancock's academic abilities. He was appointed as supervisor of a team of historians given the task of producing the twenty-eight volumes of the civil series of the official history of Britain during the war. He edited these works very closely and rewrote much of them. In 1944 Hancock was appointed Professor of Economic History at Oxford, an appointment which frequently brought him to London. Here, alongside his work on the war history and his work at Oxford, he found time to join the fire-watching service at St Paul's Cathedral, spending every Wednesday night there. It was a tiring undertaking, but Hancock thought the fellowship of the volunteers - most of them professional men like himself - to be 'the best club in London'.

In the heady days after the end of the war, a major new teaching and research institute was planned for Canberra, which was to become the Australian National University. Hancock was excited by the prospect of returning to his homeland to play a leading part in the Social Sciences department of this new creation, but his hopes were dashed. Another man was selected. He was to wait years before this hope would be realised.

Meanwhile, Hancock threw himself with his customary élan into other work. In 1949 he was appointed Director of the Institute of Commonwealth Studies within the University of London. As a result of his work there he was knighted in 1953 – now Sir Keith Hancock.

Following his previous consuming passion for the Commonwealth, Hancock's interest was now turning towards Africa. He was called in to break a political deadlock in Uganda, which he did with some tact. Hancock had long been intrigued by the figure of Field Marshall Jan Christian Smuts, Prime Minister, soldier and statesman of South Africa. Here, Hancock's interest in the Commonwealth, in nationalism, and in Africa all came together. The result was a masterful two-volume work, *Smuts*, completed in 1968, as well as his *Selections from the Smuts Papers* in four volumes in 1966.

Amongst the frenetic activity of those post-war years, Hancock published his autobiography, *Country and Calling*. I've already quoted extensively from it. It is, in fact, much more than an autobiography. It tells of what Gareth Evans, the former politician and academic, calls the central tension in Hancock's life – between *'country on one hand, with his intense and enduring passion, nurtured above all in his Bairnsdale childhood, for his own native soil, and calling on the other, his sense that he could only realise his professional destiny in the UK, and particularly Oxford'*. Another autobiographical work was to follow – *Professing History*, in 1976. The latter work consists of a number of essays and is much more oriented towards the craft of being a historian.

At last, after some twenty-four years, came the opportunity for Hancock to return to his homeland. The position at the Australian National University, once denied him, was now offered to him. He seized the opportunity with joy. From 1957 to 1961 he was Director of the Research School of Social Sciences at ANU, combining this with the Professorship of History, until his retirement in 1965. He set about widening the scope of research and teaching interests to make the School more oriented towards Asian and European themes, while he took on many other roles, especially in the field of broadening educational accessibility.

All Hancock's enthusiasm, learning and organising abilities were brought to bear in his appointment as the foundation chair of ANU's *Australian Dictionary of Biography*, now an indispensable tool for any researcher in Australian studies – a 'national monument', as it has been called. Dr Barry Jones has described the *Australian Dictionary of Biography* as 'our greatest collective research project in the humanities and a national triumph'. The Dictionary now consists of nineteen volumes, with more to come. The whole enterprise is available online at no cost. There are more than 13,500 entries about individuals who have contributed to the building up of our nation in all fields of endeavour. Keith Hancock's contribution has been immense. The Preface to the 12th edition acknowledged the part he played:

When Sir Keith Hancock, the most honoured of Australian historians, died on 13 August 1988 in his ninety-first year, he had seen ten volumes of the Australian Dictionary of Biography appear, and launched the tenth with a sunny speech that displayed both pride and modesty: pride in the work, modesty about his own part in creating it. The future of his creation is now so solidly assured that we can confidently expect a long entry on him in a volume as yet unnumbered.... As chairman of Editorial Board and National Committee, and as pipe-smoking neighbour, Hancock gave the general editor counsel, blessing and protection. ... The appearance of Volume 1 in 1966 was perhaps the most gratifying event in Hancock's first year of retirement. By the time he launched Volume 10, twenty years later, he was sure that the makers of the A.D.B. had not only made good their ambition to produce a work comparable with the British model, but had done better.

In recognition of his work on this project, Hancock received a second knighthood, this time on the nomination of the Australian government.

Hancock lived a very active retirement over more than twenty years. His wife, Thea, had died in 1960, and shortly afterwards he married his long-standing research assistant, Marjorie Eyre. He kept his hand in at the university. He became the inaugural president of the Australian Academy of the Humanities. He'd attend seminars in his old department, contributing, one observer noted, 'mellow recollection and constructive advice'.

He took a lively interest in local affairs. When the civic fathers of Canberra proposed to place a communication tower on Black Mountain, Hancock fought (unsuccessfully) 'in full cantankerous fox-terrier mode' to oppose it. He entered the lists against having American bases on Australian soil. (Generally speaking, Hancock was against almost everything American!) He came out strongly against nuclear power and nuclear weapons. On a gentler note, Hancock would appear each year as captain of the Institute of Advanced Studies cricket team in their annual match against the School of General Studies, and when he felt himself too old to play, he took up umpiring the match.

In his later years Hancock moved towards a greater concern for environmental matters and also Australian aboriginal history and culture. These two interests came together in his *Discovering Monaro*, published in 1972 when Hancock was seventy-four. Free from the need to observe the niceties of academic discourse, Hancock wrote naturally and freely from the heart. The personality of the man is more accessible here than in his earlier scholarly writing. He followed his own prescription of 'walking the ground', tramping the tablelands and high country of the Monaro and yarning to the old settlers. In his own words,

In Monaro much of my work has been done in the open air. In the summer I have walked in the high country; in the winter I have walked through paddocks on the tableland. Knowledgeable and agreeable companions have taught me how to use my eyes in both landscapes.

Discovering Monaro remains a classic work in its methodology and its environmental purpose. It includes broad principles and down-to-earth information. From it, for instance, I myself learnt fine distinctions, such as that Michelago, between Canberra and Cooma, is the place where the dominance of the white-backed magpie gives way to that of the black-backed magpie! At quite a different level, Professor DA Low describes the work as 'arguably the primary fillip to the study of Australian environmental history to this day', while the book's publisher claims, justly, that

Discovering Monaro, a fascinating local history of an Australian region, is at the same time a contribution to the current debate on the environment and man's manipulation of it. He discovers in Monaro, as he did on the terraced hillsides of Tuscany forty years ago, a rhythm of spoiling, restoring and improving. Monaro, a region of nearly 6,000 square miles in Australia's south-eastern corner, is the main provider of water to the earth's driest continent. Sir Keith provides a detailed history of the land use of the area from palaeolithic times to the present day, thus explaining how 600 generations of 'black' Australians and six generations of 'white' Australians have supported themselves on its grassy uplands and alpine water-sheds.

The memories of his boyhood days in Bairnsdale haunted Hancock all his days. Towards the end he planned to return to the scene of his boyhood and drink once more at the fountain that had sustained him over his long years. But as Jim Davidson goes on:

There was one return journey he never made: to Bairnsdale. He had proposed in 1981 that a group of contemporaries should hire a houseboat on the Gippsland Lakes ...but he had left it too late. They were not up to it. ... Now Bob Gollan was prepared to drive him there, and it was arranged, but Hancock pulled out. ... Nonetheless he urged him to go to Bairnsdale regardless and find out what he could about Ronnie Dahlsen, the boy he had rescued from the river over seventy years before. The Gollans duly went and reported that they had come across some Dahlsen relatives. The boy who in gratitude had offered Keith all that he had in his money box was now the owner of a number of country stores.

Sir Keith Hancock died in August, 1988, in Canberra Hospital, aged ninety. Michael Thwaites, the celebrated poet, was a friend of Hancock's and, like Hancock, a man of the New South Wales tablelands. On Hancock's death, Thwaites wrote a superb poem for him. The concluding stanzas are shown here:

Taking Leave

For Keith Hancock

In the hospital by the lake, where white men first built huts,

a frail old man lies waiting the final lifting of light,

frail frame, but the sinewy mind chafes the expended body,

ready to travel further, time to be up and away.

Ninety years youthful, questing through generations,

historian of two hemispheres, quickener of other minds,

lover of your own country, Gippsland to the Monaro,

searching with fearless beam the fate of humankind,

this travailed world your span: but home in the end was here.

Clear voice, warm friend, farewell. A cloud beyond our guess

goes with you over the ranges to another country and calling,

to a fellowship of all souls, to a light we cannot see.

Hancock was awarded an Order of Merit by the Italian Republic. He had honours conferred on him on four continents. Nine universities conferred honorary doctorates upon him. The Science Library at ANU is named in his honour. He was the 1973 Boyer Lecturer. The Australian Historical Association awards a biennial WK Hancock prize recognising a first scholarly book in a historical field. Two portraits – by June Mendoza and Frances Philip – are held at the ANU, and a bust by Alan Jarvis is at the Institute of Commonwealth Studies in London. I know of no memorials to him in Gippsland.

Professor Noel Butlin gave the eulogy at Sir Keith's funeral, saying, in part:

Keith was a highly intelligent, cultured, generous and kindly man with an innate simplicity. He was lively and witty, even sometimes naughty. But in all his work, in his relations with colleagues and subordinates and in his administrative activities, he is properly described as a true Christian in all the best and none of the bad senses of the word.

BERTHA McNAMARA

... who lived quietly in Bairnsdale for many years and went on to become one of the nation's foremost radicals and feminists, known as 'the Little Mother of Australian Labor'.

Matilda Emilie Bertha Kalkstein came from her native homeland, Prussia, to live with her relatives, the Drevermanns, in Bairnsdale, in 1869. The Drevermanns were a notable family in the town from its earliest days. Bertha was sixteen and her duties were to look after the Drevermann children. Her mind was not always on the children, however, for three years later, aged nineteen, she married Peter Hermann Bredt at St John's Church. Mr Bredt, a fellow-Prussian, was employed as Secretary to the local Council.

Peter Bredt was a very good Shire Secretary, renowned for his thoroughness and accuracy. The couple had nine children, although three of them died in infancy. And then, in 1888, after sixteen years of marriage, the father died, too, leaving Bertha, at thirty-five, a widow with that large young family. Until then, Bertha seems to have been an unremarkable young woman, devoted only to her family. Things were to change!

Soon after her husband's death, Bertha took her family to Melbourne where she found work as a saleswoman, at first selling jewellery and, later on, sewing machines. Her mind, again, was running on other things, for, just two or three years later, she wrote and published a pamphlet criticising the capitalist system and advocating State socialism. The pamphlet was entitled, *Home Talk on Socialism*.

This was in 1891. Socialism was a prominent issue in those pre-Federation days, although it had little direction, its tone being universal and utopian rather than directly political. The American Socialist, Edward Bellamy, had a huge influence here. It was under his influence that the extraordinary venture of 'New Australia' occurred. In 1893, 238 idealistic Australians sailed to Paraguay to found a new Socialist enclave there. Bellamy's ideas deeply influenced Bertha Bredt also.

The movement that came to be known as socialism grew from the wretched conditions endured by many people in the industrialised conditions of nineteenth century Britain and Europe. The world Dickens created through his novels depicting the squalor and hopelessness of many people in England conveys the scene in popular imagination. In rejection of the capitalist system which brought about such conditions, many longed for a society in which all might share equally. The socialist programme provided such thinkers with a way forward. Socialism is famously defined as a theory of social organisation which advocates that 'the means of production, distribution, and exchange' should be owned and regulated by society as a whole.

We can appreciate how early and how significant Bertha's maiden publication was. It is indeed a remarkable document, one of the first publications pleading the Socialist cause to be published in Australia. It is a mere nine pages in length and only one copy is known still to exist – in the Mitchell Library in Sydney. Bertha writes with a keen sense of drama and persuasion, all the more remarkable as English was not her native tongue:

Even from where I am writing I can see a grand palatial residence, the beautiful grounds whereon it stands are sloping right down to a lovely river bank, with the mild autumn sun shining upon it—Eden itself could scarce have looked fairer .... Its owner has gone to live in another beautiful mansion near a large city, where he and his family can enjoy the gaiety of the winter season. He soweth not, neither does he reap, neither does he make himself otherwise useful, he is an independent gentleman of a large fortune. Only a short distance from this beautiful mansion, are a number of small cottages, more or less in preservation, mostly less, here the labourers live with their families, the men who toil, who sow, and who reap, to provide the rich man and his kindred with bread; the men who, to the best of their strength and ability, do their share of life's labour. Here they live, with wife and children, huddled together in a few small rooms and even these are the rich man's property.

Bertha goes on to write about the cruel treatment given to the shearers who were then engaged in the notorious 1891 shearers' strike in Queensland.

Government under the control of Capital has, under the plea of keeping law and order, sent out its soldiery to aid one section of the community against the other. ... Who would not be a Socialist, and help with might and strength to build a social structure where strife and fighting would cease?

Bertha had now met William McNamara, a pioneer of Socialist agitation in Australia, and whom she married in the following year, 1892. William, the son of Irish parents, was one of a small group of men who had founded the Australian Socialist League a few years earlier, and had gone on to work for the Shearers' Union. Tall, dark, and bearded, he cut an impressive figure, and was a brilliant public speaker and union organizer. He pulled no punches. After publishing a pamphlet against the banks, he was found guilty of libel and sent to prison for a short spell. This was the background to Bertha's developing involvement in the Labor movement.

Soon after, the McNamaras moved to Sydney where two more children were born and where Bertha spent the rest of her life. Bertha threw herself into local radical affairs. Becoming disaffected with the Australian Socialist League, she and William founded the Social Democratic Federation of Australasia. Three more pamphlets flowed from her pen. Broadly, the position she argued was that a Socialist state must be built up from grass-roots community change rather than being imposed by political action from above. This led to a split from the more extreme side of the radical movement in later years.

By the mid-1890s Bertha's family ranged from those in their 'twenties down to a one-year-old - and there was one more child yet to be born. In 1896 two of her daughters, Bertha and Hilda, were married. Both married men destined to be famous. Bertha married Henry Lawson who gained fame as the great Australian writer and bush poet, while Hilda married John Thomas Lang – 'Jack' or 'the Big Fella', as he was commonly known – who would become Premier of New South Wales and a highly divisive figure in the Labor movement in the 'twenties and 'thirties. He is best remembered by many because of the incident in 1932 when, as Premier, he opened the Sydney Harbour Bridge, although beaten to it by Major De Groot who rode up on horseback and slashed the ribbon before it could receive the official treatment by the Premier. Despite his commanding presence, Lang remained in awe – some say, fear – of his mother-in-law!

However, Bertha's fame at that time lay in a different direction. She and William established a bookshop in Castlereagh Street, Sydney, that became the centre of radical and progressive thinking for the next thirty years. After William's death in 1906, Bertha carried it on alone. Known as the Progressive Book Depot, it was also a lending library and reading room. Verity Burgmann, in the *Australian Dictionary of Biography*, writes:

Bertha ran a boarding house in conjunction with the shop. Practical and kind, she fed and housed many new migrants from Europe until they found employment. The back room and the reading room above the shop were scenes of almost constant activity and discussion by socialists, feminists, anarchists, rationalists, Laborites and literary Bohemians.

The poet, Roderic Quinn, years later, spoke nostalgically of the days of Bertha's bookshop:

There was E. J. Brady, storming with revolution, and Fred Broomfield, father of the Bohemians. .... There was Victor Daly, and last, but not least, Henry Lawson. We went there for intellectual entertainment, and a quiet hour. We were idealists in those days and dreamt dreams...

At about the same time, the *Australian Worker* also looked back in cheerful reminiscence:

Amongst the many who made [Bertha's] house their more or less constant or frequent Mecca in the earlier days of the NSW sector of the Labor Movement were Messrs WM Hughes, WA Holman, and then later Messrs McTiernan, Sproule, the late Percy Brookfield, and amongst the visitors, Henry Lawson (her son-in-law), Tom Mann, Harry Holland and Bob Ross. Other men who are now Judges, leading journalists, or otherwise in the limelight, took a delight in browsing among her books or listening to her conversation.

For a glimpse of Bertha herself in those days, we turn to an article in the *Sun* published in December, 1922. We must understand that Bertha retained her thick German accent all her life.

It is a familiar resort in Castlereagh-street, this depot of terrific literature. All sorts of cheerful foreign gentlemen and amiable conspirators have stalked in and out of its little, narrow door in the years when anarchy was a hobby of much the same calibre as chess or dominoes. It is going to be pulled down. ... In a few weeks, the old window filled with scarlet propaganda will have vanished. Mrs McNamara is disconsolate, but in her sorrow she still has dreams of the old anarchists and ancient Nihilists and the queer visitors who came to thumb her books ... twenty years ago.

A young man with eager eyes and head slightly on one side stood apologetically at the door. "I say, Mrs McNamara," he began, "can I— can I borrow a table and some chairs?" "Vat? Anooza meeteeng?" "It's only a little one," said the young man hurriedly. "I think they're going to make me secretary." "Zen, ze table, eet ees yours," consented Mrs McNamara, "and ze chairs? Of vat use are ze chairs when one may ave ze table, and speak on 'im? But 'ave ze chairs, mon bravo — and bring zem back." The young man dragged the table and chairs off to a little room above some long-forgotten lane, and the little meeting was held. Mrs McNamara says she thinks the chairs were brought back.

He was rather a remarkable young man, this borrower of innumerable chairs and tables. He was very small and active, spoke well, thought quickly, heard badly, dressed carelessly, and sometimes told people to go to "blithering blazes". You have guessed it. He was William Morris Hughes. Does he ever remember McNamara's bookshop now? Ask Mrs McNamara. "Vat? Beely? Eem? 'E ees not von of us. Ve do not care zat for eem."* *Mrs McNamara snapped her fingers melodramatically.*

(*Billy Hughes later 'ratted' on the Labor Party.)

The bookshop *was* pulled down ... but Bertha moved to another building and then another, then back to another place in Castlereagh Street. She was indomitable! Stinging pamphlets continued from her hand, with titles such as, *Commercialism and Distribution of the Nineteenth Century, Forgery, Workingmen's Homes, How to become rich beyond the Dreams of Avarice, Paper Money,* and *Shylock Exposed.* To take just one as an example, *Shylock Exposed* was another thin booklet, just seven pages, and bore an alternative title – *Usury, its curse and its cure.* It declared itself to be 'a timely discussion of the phenomena attending the collapse of capitalism with suggestions for hastening the same'.

The position of women in society in the late nineteenth century was demeaning in the extreme. They had no legal rights over their children, educational opportunities were restricted, they received wages much lower than men's, divorce was almost impossible, they had no vote, and played subsidiary roles to their husbands in almost every field of life, from banking and commerce to their children's education. There was a lively movement in New South Wales working to improve this situation. It came to be realised that the key to change was for women to be given the vote. Out of a cluster of women's improvement societies, the Womanhood Suffrage League of New South Wales was born. Bertha McNamara was one of the key members, alongside many other well-known women, including Louisa Lawson, Henry Lawson's mother. The campaign eventually succeeded. Women in NSW achieved the vote in 1902, nine years after South Australia, but six years before Victoria. Bertha herself was nominated for pre-selection for the Federal Senate in 1928. If she had been elected she would have been the first woman to enter the Australian Federal parliament. It took another fifteen years for the first women to be elected to Canberra.

When the First World War broke out, the Bookshop became busier than ever. Bertha stocked anti-militarist publications even though they were banned by the government. When WM Hughes tried to introduce conscription, Bertha's shop became a stronghold of anti-conscription propaganda and activity.

In 1931, a peculiar combination of events took place. The first was the unveiling of a statue of Henry Lawson in the Sydney Domain. Bertha, his mother-in-law, however, was ill and unable to attend. She had gone out to 'have words' with another woman activist with whom she disagreed, caught pneumonia, and was admitted to hospital. Then, a few days later, a hostel for unemployed women and girls was opened in Central Sydney. This was at a time when the Great Depression was first taking hold in Australia and unemployment was increasing. The hostel was named the 'Bertha McNamara Hostel' in honour of Bertha and her contribution to the Labor movement over forty years. Ironically and sadly, Bertha was still in hospital. A close friend of Bertha's and fellow-activist, Mrs RJ Cassidy, spoke on the occasion:

It is befitting that this hostel should be named after Mrs McNamara for everybody wholeheartedly agrees that this fine old lady should be monumented, not when she is dead, but while, happily, she is still among us – though not here today in person ...I think that Mrs McNamara, in a Labor sense, might well be termed the 'Mother of the Movement' ... Mrs McNamara did not baulk at difficulties. She knew that some day the workers who create the wealth of the country would at least – and at last – have Parliamentary control of the country. And what has happened since shows how right were her vision and her prophecy. ... Thousands throughout the country, while deploring the necessity for such an institution will gratefully remember the grand old lady whose honoured name it bears.

The culmination of this trilogy of events was the death of Bertha herself. She died in hospital on 1 August, 1931, days after the opening of her hostel. The news was carried in newspapers across the nation. Tributes poured in from all over Australia. The tone of these tributes is perhaps best summed up in the words of the *Adelaide Advertiser*, that 'when the history of the Labor Party in New South Wales and in Australia is written her name will loom large'. The funeral was conducted by Mr J Bowden from the

Rationalist Association, who described Bertha as 'an idealist in the highest and best sense of the word'.

A fine tribute to Bertha was made a few months later. A bronze tablet commemorating Bertha's life and work was placed in the Entrance Foyer of Trades Hall in Sydney. It consists of an embossed bust of Bertha done by the celebrated artist, Lyndon Dadswell, with her name and these words engraved below:

> *Kindly and gracious in her splendid way,*
> *She knew no nationhood.*
> *And her religion each and every day*
> *Was that of doing good.*

A large crowd attended the event. Mrs Lena Lynch, in unveiling the tablet, said, in part, 'She was the grand old lady and mother of the Labor movement. She was no summer soldier or sunshine patriot. Her work and life were devoted to the Labor movement'.

We might reflect on whether Bertha, in her later life, mixing with the leaders of our national intellectual and political life, allowed herself to think back to those old days when, as a sixteen-year-old immigrant, she found herself walking the streets of Bairnsdale, accustoming herself to the ways of this new land. Could she have glimpsed what lay in store for her?

We conclude by turning once more to the nature of the woman herself. Michael Richards, in a perceptive essay in *Diversity in Leadership: Australian Women Past and Present*, has included the words Bertha's daughter, Clarice, said of her mother as she spoke about the famous Castlereagh Street bookshop:

No picture in my memory could be clearer than those overcrowded shelves bulging with lively books and journals, and behind the counter the compelling personality of the little proprietress. No-one who did not know her would have guessed, from her sparkling periwinkle-blue eyes, her beautiful skin and soft white hair and her general air of maternal tenderness mixed with a lovely sense of fun, that this was one of the most dogged fighters for human rights and social justice in the history of Australian politics.

LIONEL ROSE

...who grew up in humble circumstances at Jindivick and became a World boxing champion, mixing with the greats, and won awards and accolades around Australia and the world.

In his song, 'Jackson's Track', Lionel Rose sings of growing up in 'the buses and the tumble-down shacks' on the ad hoc Aboriginal settlement that formed around Daryl Tonkin's saw-mill on Jackson's Track in Jindivick, north of Drouin. The settlement itself became known, simply, as 'Jackson's Track'.

There is no sense in Lionel of deprivation or mistreatment. Lionel Rose was like that. He took himself and the people he came across with calm acceptance. The story of the enforced breaking-up of the Jackson's Track settlement is a tragic one and has been well documented in the book of that name written by Carolyn Landon and Daryl Tonkin himself. None of the bitterness, however, got into Lionel Rose's soul.

The women at the Jackson's Track camp were the ones who held the people together and who maintained a sense of community and also discipline. One of them was Lionel's mother, Regina. In May, 2023, a statue was unveiled in Civic Park, Drouin, of three of those women – Regina Rose, Lionel's mother, Dora Hood, Lionel's grandmother, and Euphemia Mullet, Daryl Tonkin's wife. At the time Lionel was growing up in the basic conditions of the camp, little would it have been thought that one day there would be a statue of Regina Rose in Drouin and a statue of her son, Lionel, in nearby Warragul.

Lionel had very limited formal education. He started school when he was eight. That involved walking three miles to the Labertouche school, but he stayed home as much as he went to school. Two years later, when the camp was broken up, the Rose family (Lionel had seven brothers and sisters) was moved into Drouin, to a two-bedroom house, but attending school was not a priority for Lionel. In fact, his father, Roy, was fined – and even sent to prison, briefly – for the truancy of his children. Later in life, in Melbourne, Lionel made a point of improving his literacy, encouraged by his trainer's wife, Shirley Rennie.

Lionel had that kind of trusting personality that older people readily took an interest in him and gave him a hand. One of the first to do so was Graham Walsh. When Lionel was ten, in 1958, he was chosen to go to Melbourne with three others on a trip sponsored by the Save the Children Fund. Graham Walsh was the photographer assigned to cover the trip. He had once boxed himself and, learning of Lionel's feeling for boxing, gave him an old set of gloves and took him to some training sessions and to see some bouts in Melbourne.

Lionel's father, Roy, also pushed him towards boxing. Roy had done some boxing in the sideshow tents at local shows. Older people will remember them. A group of boxers, many Aboriginal, would be lined up outside the tent while the promoter goaded the local youths into going a few rounds with one of their own weight. Once a local accepted the challenge, a crowd would pour into the tent (at a cost!) to cheer on their champion, not often with happy results!

Lionel had his first bout – as an amateur – in Sale when he was twelve years old. At this time, he was involved with the Warragul Youth Club, and it was one of the men who ran the Club, Dave Proctor, who arranged that fight. Lionel lost against a taller and heavier opponent. It was some time before he returned to the ring. After leaving school (officially) at fourteen in 1962, he worked spasmodically at various unskilled jobs around the district. He worked at a sawmill for some months, then in a laundry and also in a welding business. His work ethic, by his own admission, was not good. Later, in Melbourne, in training but before his boxing career took off, he had a variety of jobs, but failed to stick at any of them. His dedication to boxing was of a different order.

The next people to give Rose a helping hand towards his later spectacular career were Frank and Nerida Oakes. The Oakes were well known and respected figures in Warragul. Frank was a railway man, his wife the High School librarian. Frank was a knockabout footballer – he played for Bunyip and Warragul, and went on to coach the Warragul Thirds. He was also something of a boxer. The Oakes were wonderful mentors to the teenager. Indeed, their lives became aligned with Rose's as he was later to marry their daughter, Jenny. Frank Oakes trained Rose for his first fights. It was under Oakes that Rose won the national amateur flyweight title (for boxers between 49 kg and 51 kg) at Festival Hall in Melbourne in 1963. He was fifteen years old. As Rose's brilliance progressed, Oakes introduced him to the famed Melbourne boxing coach, Jack Rennie. The next year Rose moved to Melbourne to live with the Rennies in Essendon. At the same time he turned professional. Shirley Rennie helped Rose with his speech and language and enrolled him in correspondence courses in Maths and English. She became a mother figure to him.

In 1964, just turned sixteen, Rose was runner-up to Bill Booth for the national amateur bantamweight title (between 52.2 kg and 53.5 kg), and thus narrowly missed selection for the Olympic Games in Tokyo. In September, 1964, Stadiums Limited in Melbourne arranged his first professional bout – against Mario Magriss – which he won. Over the next two years, Rose had nineteen professional fights, winning seventeen and losing two. Then, in October, 1966, now eighteen, he won the Australian bantamweight title from Noel Kunde on points in a 15-round bout, at Melbourne's Festival Hall, despite losing the last five rounds. 'He had a good left and a good straight right,' Kunde commented later.

Rose defended his national bantamweight title only once, defeating Rocky Gattellari on a knockout – a rare result for Rose - in the 13th round at Sydney Stadium. That was in December, 1967. It was the first boxing match to be televised throughout Australia. Rose gave up the national title on winning the world crown two months later.

For Australians, Rose's defeat of Fighting Harada in Tokyo in February, 1968, to win the World bantamweight championship is arguably the most significant and best-remembered bout of the century. Harada was a very experienced boxer; he'd defended his title successfully many times before. Let's take the report of the *Sydney Morning Herald* to convey the atmosphere of the occasion:

Tokyo, Tuesday: Australia's 20-year-old Lionel Rose tonight was mobbed by excited Japanese fight fans after he had taken the world bantamweight title from Japan's Fighting Harada. Hundreds of Japanese fans rushed to shower their praise on Rose as police forced a passage for him to the dressing-room.

A clear winner on points, Rose had become the first Aboriginal and only the second Australian to win an official world boxing title. Out-boxing his opponent, Rose won clearly under Australian methods of scoring, but the official result was close. The referee, Ko Toyama, gave it to Rose 72-71, judge Hiroyiiki Tezaki favoured Rose 72-69, and the other judge, Ken Morita, made it a 70-all draw. This was the first time an all-Japanese set of officials had controlled a world title bout.

When a decision was announced, Rose's manager, Jack Rennie, clasped his boxer so excitedly that the pair tumbled into midring and crashed to the canvas. Australian fight fans, who had flown to

Tokyo on special flights, invaded the ring and police had to clear many away to prevent it from collapsing.

"Don't worry," Rose told manager Rennie at the end of the third round, "he can't hit hard enough to hurt me." Rose finished the fight with a bruised knuckle on his right hand, but facially was unmarked. He hurt his right in the 14th round when he made Harada's sturdy legs stutter.

For such a young fighter, Rose was remarkably cool as he sat in his dressing-room awaiting the contest, and he cracked jokes with a few Australians present until called to the ring. "Harada is a great champion, and although I thought I could win most of the way, I was not really certain until the 14th round," Rose said. "Then he weakened for the first time in the fight and I thought I'd done enough to win by the end of the 15th," added the new champion.

Rose was repeatedly spoken to by referee Toyama and this provided the only concern for the Australian camp and its followers. Afterwards, Rennie said that the referee kept telling Rose he would have to fight more or lose the contest. This was because Rose was fighting on the retreat, and although scoring with much greater frequency than Harada, his skilful display was not suiting the referee.

"I did not feel strange in the ring, and it was just another big fight for me," said Rose. "The Aussie barrackers, with their flags and their vocal support, made it really good. A couple of times I looked *around and I could see them waving the flag, and I knew I was not in there on my own," Rose said.*

Rose, with Rennie and Mrs Shirley Rennie, leave for home tomorrow night by air. ... "I'm the happiest person in the world at the moment," Rose said. "I thought if I could last the first eight rounds I would win, and that worked out right."

Then came the return to Melbourne. The daily papers shrieked from their front pages: *"Yippee!"*, *"Hail Rose the Hero!"*, *"The Warrior Comes Home!"*, *"Lionel is the World Champ!"*, *"Champion Home!"* On landing at Essendon, Lionel saw the crowds and, in all innocence, asked an air hostess, "Are the Beatles on the plane, too?" The streets into town were lined with fans. Some estimated the crowd at 100,000, some 250,000. They arrived at the Town Hall to an official reception. 10,000 crowded around.

Public honours followed swiftly. He was appointed Australian of the Year for 1968, and in the New Year honours list was made a Member of the Order of the British Empire (MBE). Other honours flowed in. Rose was inducted into the National Boxing Hall of Fame and the Victorian Aboriginal Honour Roll. He received a Deadly Award for a Lifetime Achievement in Sport. His boxing gloves were featured on a 50-cent stamp.

Much was made of Rose's Aboriginality. Black people around the country felt a thrill of pride that one of their own had become the first Australian to win a World boxing title and was the first recognised Aboriginal world champion in any sport. Archie Roach, the Aboriginal singer and cultural hero, spoke later about the excitement of listening to Rose fighting on the radio and being told 'This man who's fighting, he's your people'. The Aboriginal man-of-affairs, Warren Mundine, called Rose his boyhood hero, and described how he and his family 'screamed and yelled and danced around the room' when Rose beat Harada for the World title. Some have likened Rose's success to that of Joe Louis, the African-American heavyweight champion of an earlier era, in that both helped to lift their people to greater pride in themselves. Stan Grant, the Aboriginal journalist, has written, in this vein:

When my brother was a young boy he was asked in class what he wanted to be when he grew up.
"Lionel Rose," he answered.

The Aboriginal world boxing champion was a hero in our family. For Aboriginal people like us, sport was a pathway to success. We did not know anyone who had been to university, but we knew a lot of boxers and footballers.

Rose defended his world title four times over the next eighteen months. The first brought him back to Tokyo to fight Takao Sakurai, a gold medallist from the 1964 Olympic Games. Rose was knocked down in the second round, but recovered to win on points. His next defence was against Chucho Castillo in Inglewood, California. Again, Rose won on points, but the decision upset the home crowd so much they rioted. Fifteen people were hospitalised in the melee, including the referee. Rose had his supporters, however. Hollywood stars Frank Sinatra and Burt Lancaster came to watch him fight. Elvis Presley was a big fan. Wendy Lewis in her *Australians of the Year* tells of Rose's reaction when Elvis came to visit:

You know what? I was punching a heavy bag in a gym in LA, and I hear a voice sing out, 'Hey Lionel! What's doin'?' And it was Elvis himself. He was making 'Roustabout'. I was in awe of him, but he said he was in awe of me.

With Jack Rennie he spent three hours on the set of the film, and sparred with the rock-and-roll hero. Beside this memory, Rose took home $75,000 as his prize money.

In March, 1969, Rose's challenger was the Briton, Alan Rudkin. The fight was at the Kooyong Tennis Centre, and the referee was Vic Patrick, who, until the advent of Rose, was the most celebrated of all Australian boxers. The report of the fight from Associated Press reads:

World bantamweight champion Lionel Rose of Australia retained his title today, hammering out a 15 round split decision over challenger Alan Rudkin of Great Britain. Rose peppered Rudkin with punches in the early rounds, scoring heavily in the 6th, but as the fight continued Rudkin picked up strength and made his best showing in the last round. The champion dominated the first seven rounds of the bout, and then tailed off badly.

In August came Rose's last title defence. Returning to California, Rose was matched with the Mexican, Reuben Olivares. Rose was knocked out in the fifth round. In the words of one commentator,

Reuben Olivares puts on an electrifying and awesomely destructive performance when he dethrones a weight-drained Lionel Rose from his crown by handing out one of the most comprehensive beatings ever seen in a world fight.

Rose was battling with his weight. He continued to box in higher weight divisions, eventually reaching world ranking in the junior lightweight division. After losing in a World title bout in June, 1971, he retired. Four years later he made an ill-advised comeback, but with little success and he gave the game away finally in 1976. He was twenty-eight.

Rose had another career of sorts – country music. He produced several records, which can all be found on the internet. His best track was probably, *'I thank you'*, a Johnny Young song, which topped the country music charts. Other songs of Rose's were *'Jackson's Track'*, *'Please remember me'* and *'Pick me up on your way down'*. Lionel first appeared on TV in 1969, singing "*Pick me up on your way down*" on variety show *Sunny Side Up*, accompanying himself on the guitar. Just as there was a great gulf between Lionel Rose and Elvis Presley as boxers, there was probably a greater gulf between them as singers!

Rose's years after he'd hung up his gloves were years of decline. Although he amassed a considerable sum through boxing and had invested in several businesses, these later years were marked by unsavoury involvement in gambling and drinking. He crossed swords with the law on several occasions.

The official Victorian state government tribute to Rose ends in this way:

Although he had his fair share of personal setbacks later in life, it is for his achievements in the ring, along with his good nature, positive outlook and generosity that he remains best remembered. In testament to the enduring affection Australians felt for Lionel, a state funeral was held upon his death in May 2011. He not only gave this country one of its most inspiring modern stories of triumph against the odds, he deservedly earned himself the title of 'Australian Hero'.

Commenting on Rose after his death, Frank Quill, a World Boxing Council official, brought out a little-known aspect of Rose's conduct. The newspaper report read:

... Frank Quill said Rose was a fantastic world champion and one of the first sports identities to make a stand against Apartheid-ravaged South Africa.

"He became world champion at a time when, in two or three states of Australia, Aboriginal people weren't entitled to vote," an emotional Quill, president of the WBC's ratings committee, told

AAP on Sunday. Quill recounted Rose's refusal of a big money fight in South Africa in 1970. The offer came not long after Rose had lost his world title to the Mexican, Rueben Olivares, and at a time when he was almost certainly in need of money.

"He considered the fight and if he had have taken it he would have had to go there (South Africa) as an "honorary white", Quill said.

So he said: 'I'm not going'. To my knowledge he was the first sportsman to refuse to go to South Africa because of Apartheid.

Lionel Rose died at his home in Warragul on 8th May, 2011, aged sixty-two. He is buried in the Warragul Cemetery. The Fox Sports report of the State Funeral is a fitting way to end this summary of Rose's life and achievements:

Among the mourners at the state funeral were Rose's long-time trainer Jack Rennie, who attended in a wheelchair, former world champion Johnny Famechon and Aboriginal fighter Tony Mundine.

Federal Sports Minister Mark Arbib, former Victorian premier John Brumby and Opposition Leader Daniel Andrews were also at the hall where Rose fought 23 professional fights. ...

Aboriginal elder Aunty Joy said Rose excelled in the boxing ring at a young age and showed the world the tenacity and integrity of a young Aboriginal man.

"He knew from an early age the challenges facing his family and the Aboriginal community," Aunty Joy told mourners.

"Lionel's career has been an inspiration for many," she said. "Lionel will be remembered making history and receiving recognition at the tender age of 19. Those momentous times were celebrated with enormous pride. Lionel also sent a strong message especially to young people around the world to stand up and fight for your rights and aspire to reach your dream."

Victorian Premier Ted Baillieu said Rose would forever be remembered as one of Victoria's greatest champions and a national treasure. "There was, and remains, only one Lionel," Mr Baillieu told mourners. "People genuinely loved him and felt protective of him. He was a thoroughly decent and gentle soul. He inspired us, he charmed us, and he in turn grew up with us."...

Rose's god-daughter Bonnie Anderson sang the Eagles hit 'Desperado' at the service.

SIR STANLEY SAVIGE

...a Morwell boy - and later Wonthaggi - who served valiantly in two world wars, saved the lives of thousands of Assyrian refugees, and founded Legacy, one of the nation's major outreach organisations.

We could have four separate chapters on Stanley Savige. He was something of a hero in the First World War and again in the Second World War. At the tail end of the First War he saved 50,000 Assyrian refugees from slaughter, and then he came back home to found Legacy, which is his continuing gift to the Australian nation.

Both Morwell and Wonthaggi lay claim to Stan Savige. He was born in Morwell in 1890, and there is a memorial to him there, His family moved to Wonthaggi when he was seven and Stan went to the Wonthaggi State school, and there is a memorial to him there, as well. Really, however, Savige belongs to the nation.

Stan's first years can be briefly told. He was brought up in the hard days of the 1890s Depression, the oldest of eight children. His father built the family home himself from bush planks hewed and trimmed with his own hands. Stan left school early and worked for a blacksmith before going on to several other unskilled jobs. His family moved from Wonthaggi to Prahran when he was seventeen, and Stan began a three-year teacher-training course. He had been a member of the Junior Cadets before that, and became a leader in the new adventure organisation, the Boy Scouts, which Lord Baden Powell had founded just a few years earlier, in 1908. Stan was fond of the outdoors and enjoyed roughing it. He was also a Sunday School teacher in the South Yarra Baptist Church, and had some notion of entering the church ministry. The church has since moved; the building Stan knew (and where he was later married) is now a pub! Not long before the First World War broke out, he became engaged to Miss Lilian Stockton.

Savige enlisted in March, 1915, and was posted to the 24th Battalion, 6th Infantry Brigade. In September he arrived on Gallipoli and saw service particularly at Lone Pine where he became known as a crack sniper. He rose rapidly through the ranks. By now the Gallipoli campaign was winding down. In the last days, Savige was put in command of one of the rearguard parties. In a brilliant operation the bloodless evacuation was completed at 4.00 am on 20 December. Savige was in the last group to leave.

The 24th Battalion went on to serve in France at Pozieres and Mouquet Farm. By now commissioned as Lieutenant Savige, he was in charge of the Battalion's scout platoon, which saw him leading night-time reconnaissance patrols into no-man's-land. From there he was seconded into the Brigade Commander's Intelligence office. The Brigade Commander was Brigadier-General John Gellibrand who was deeply impressed by Savige's work. The friendship between the two men lasted in war and peace for many years. Savige was promoted to Captain and shortly afterwards, in January, 1917, returned as Adjutant – administrative officer - to the 24th Battalion.

On 3 May, the 6th Brigade played a major role in the Second Battle of Bullecourt. This was one of the bloodiest days of the war for the Australians, losing 7,500 killed or wounded. The Brigade found itself in a precarious position. They advanced deep into the German lines and held on grimly, but were in danger of being outflanked. Savige was in the leading trench, coordinating the defence against German counter-attacks. His actions led to his being recommended for a Military Cross for conspicuous gallantry, in that he displayed 'commendable coolness, energy and ability'. However, the award was never promulgated. Savige was 'Mentioned in Dispatches' instead, and had to wait until January, 1918 to be awarded an MC. Then, the citation added that he displayed 'coolness under fire and tenacity of purpose'.

Savige next saw action at the Battle of Passchendaele several months later. Here he was Mentioned in Dispatches a second time. It is worth recording the whole of this citation:

For conspicuous gallantry. On the night of the 3rd/4th Oct he assisted in laying out jumping-off and direction tapes at Zonnebeke on which the attacking battalions formed up. He then checked their correctness. This was done under heavy fire. He then helped to guide the attackers to their positions. On the night 8th/9th October he did similar work on Broodseinde Ridge under particularly heavy fire, and throughout the attack on the 9th October he remained in the forward area gathering information and forwarding it to Brigade Headquarters. This Officer has been on many occasions conspicuous for his gallantry.

Here the second chapter on Stanley Savige might begin. Following the 1917 Russian Revolution, the new Bolshevik government signed a peace treaty with Germany in March, 1918, and withdrew from the war. This was an alarming development for the Allies for several reasons. Apart from relieving the German army from the difficulty of fighting on two fronts, it left open a corridor on the eastern front through which German and Turkish forces could have direct access to India, from where they could draw huge resources for their failing war effort. To counter this, the British War Office drew up a plan to send a hand-picked fighting force to 'plug the gap', hopefully with the help of straggling Russian troops and local tribesmen. This force was to be 'the cream of the cream'. Twenty Australian officers were chosen to join the force, including Captain Stanley Savige.

The unit was known as Dunsterforce, after its British commander, Major-General Lionel Dunsterville. This select force of 300 men travelled from London through France and Italy by train, then by ship through the Mediterranean and the Suez Canal to Basra at the head of the Persian Gulf. From there they made their way up the Tigris River and then overland to north-western Iran, which was then known as Persia. It was a huge logistical undertaking, carrying men, supplies, and equipment using donkey and horse transport across deserts and into precipitous mountain terrain, while living off the land for a good part of the time. Savige's particular role was to go on ahead of the main force to make contact with local guerrilla units and seek to bring them in to join the main body of troops.

Here an unexpected twist occurred, which was to make Stanley Savige's name for ever honoured. The expeditionary force came across a straggling mass of some 60,000 Christian Assyrian refugees fleeing from Persian and Kurdish forces intent on annihilating them. Many had already been killed or had died on the wayside. They made up a whole population, men, women, children, and animals, carrying their possessions, under constant attack from their rear. Savige was deeply moved by the plight of these people. With some difficulty he gained approval – some say he acted against orders – and set out to delay the hostile forces so the refugees could get to safety in Baghdad. He had just eight men with him to begin with, although he recruited some local guerrillas to bolster their numbers. The tiny group stationed themselves behind the tail of the long line of refugees to form a rearguard against attack. They used tricks to make it appear they were stronger in number, for instance by lighting a series of camp-fires at night to give the impression of a much larger force. The situation called on all Savige's strategic and personal resources. The small party succeeded in holding off the attackers until the refugee column had passed into safe territory. Perhaps 10,000 died. More than 50,000 were rescued.

Official War Historian CEW Bean wrote of this action:

The stand made by Savige and his eight companions that evening and during half of the next day against hundreds of the enemy thirsting like wolves to get at the defenceless throng was as fine as any episode known to the present writer in the history of this war.

Savige received the Distinguished Service Order for his efforts. The citation read:

For conspicuous gallantry and devotion to duty during the retirement of refugees from Sain Kelen to Tikkaa Tappah, 26/28th July, 1918; also at Chalkaman, 5/6th August. In command of a small party sent to protect the rear of the column of refugees, he by his resource and able dispositions kept off the enemy, who were in greatly superior numbers. He hung on to position after position until nearly surrounded, and on each occasion extricated his command most skilfully. His cool determination and fine example inspired his men, and put heart into the frightened refugees.

There are some 60,000 people of Assyrian descent living in Australia at the present time. The great majority of them are in Sydney, concentrated in the City of Fairfield. Many of them come from the families rescued by Savige and his small party. To them, Stanley Savige's name is hugely revered. 'Without him, we would have been wiped out,' one of them says. In Fairfield a monument to

Assyrian forces has been erected. It mentions by name two men of Dunsterforce – Sir Stanley George Savige and a New Zealander, Captain Robert Kenneth Nicol. Andrew Rohan, a former member of the NSW Parliament is a descendant of those rescued Assyrians. His mother and father were both among that chaos of fleeing refugees. He opened his inaugural speech to the NSW Parliament in 2011 by mentioning Stanley Savage and said the Assyrian community will forever be grateful for his heroic actions. 'He is not just a hero to the Assyrian community, he is a saint,' Mr Rohan said. 'Our family's existence is thanks to him and the entire Assyrian community feel the same way.'

His incredible achievements in Gallipoli and on the Western Front, and then in Persia, brought Savige to the point of complete exhaustion. He was hospitalised for weeks, and during this time the war ended. Savige returned to Melbourne to marry his patient sweetheart Lilian. In 1920 he published an account of the Dunsterforce epic entitled *Stalky's Forlorn Hope*. (The title is a complicated play on the name of the Commander, Major-General Dunsterville. When Rudyard Kipling wrote his adventure book, *Stalky and Co*, he based the main character – Stalky- on Lionel Dunsterville as a schoolboy.)

Now begins the third chapter in Stanley Savige's eventful life. Savige went into business when the war ended and did very well in the wool trade. In 1922, his old Commander, Major-General John Gellibrand, invited him to Hobart, where Gellibrand had set up a

Remembrance Club for ex-servicemen, with the aim of assisting former diggers who were having difficulties, especially in business matters. Gellibrand urged Savige to form a similar club in Melbourne. Savige did so, but when the group met in the old Anzac House in Russell Street they decided to go further and work towards caring for the widows and children of ex-servicemen as their primary task. The name, 'Legacy', was adopted. It's said that the words of a dying soldier on the Western Front -"Look after the missus and the kids" – was their spiritual motivation. The work was entirely voluntary. Savige immersed himself totally in extending the movement. He and Lilian had bought a large beach house at Somers on the Mornington Peninsula, and they made that the centre of many of the new organisation's activities.

Groups of boys and girls, separately, would stay at the house for weekends and in school holidays. Life was deliberately not made easy for them. Discipline was strict. Tasks were scheduled. Daily inspections were made. Savige's instincts developed as a scoutmaster as well as a soldier came to the fore. Although Legacy expanded beyond all expectations, Savige remained the heart and soul of it. One commentator described him as 'frenetic, fearsome and fanatical'. He went on:

His efforts were extraordinary. With belief, incredible zeal and by pure force of argument and character, but no initial capital whatsoever the organisation developed, expanded, multiplied and attended to the needs, desires, and hopes of ever increasing numbers of war widows and their children.

Legacy children marched on Anzac Day in their white uniforms. Thousands of ex-servicemen and others volunteered their time to serve as legatees. By 1930 Legacy clubs had been formed all over Australia, not just in the capital cities.

Outreach was stimulated by the outbreak of the Second World War. Legacy Week was instituted in 1942. The organisation became one of Australia's best known and most respected charities. Legacy currently supports 40,000 individuals and families across Australia, supported by over 3,400 volunteer members.

2023 marks the centenary of Legacy. On Anzac Day of this year, a Legacy Centenary Torch Relay began at Pozieres in France. It went to the battle scenes known to Stanley Savige - Bullecourt and Villers-Bretonneux – and then to the Menin Gate at Ypres, where it was displayed while the Last Post was sounded at nightfall. From there it travelled to London, to be flown to Australia. As this book goes to press the torch has just passed through Wagga Wagga en route to Sydney. From there it comes to Sale and on to Tasmania before reaching its destination at the Shrine of Remembrance in Melbourne on Friday, 13th October. That will be six months after the beginning of the Relay, and after the torch has travelled 50,000 kilometres and been carried by 1,500 torchbearers. It is expected that ten million dollars will be raised for the work of Legacy.

The fourth chapter in this remarkable man's life began when the Second World War broke out. Savige was forty-nine years of age. His business and Legacy activities had not prevented him maintaining a peace-time military career. He joined the Militias as early as 1920 and over the next nineteen years served as Commander of several Militia units, rising to the rank of Colonel and then, in 1938, Brigadier.

Savige answered the call to arms immediately on the outbreak of war. His service number was VX13. In October, 1939, he was appointed Commander of the 17th Brigade, 6th Division. This appointment of a 'citizen soldier' to such a rank was not popular with other regular officers – the professional soldiers – and this feeling was a constant shadow over Savige throughout the war. The Brigade first saw action in the Battle of Bardia in North Africa in January, 1941, and won an emphatic victory, despite some disarray within the Brigade. The 17th went on to play a minor role in the Battle of Tobruk some weeks later, and took part in the advance on Derna. Soon after, Savige was appointed Commander of the British Empire (CBE).

Savige's 17th Brigade went on to take part in the ill-fated campaign in Greece. Under incessant air attacks, the Allies were forced to retreat, then evacuate. Savige was praised for his personal bravery and was awarded the Greek Military Cross. Transferred to Syria, the Brigade was pitted against the Vichy forces which had taken over the French mandated territories there and played a part in the capture of Damour, which ended enemy resistance in the region. Savige regarded this brief campaign as his most successful single operation for the whole war. He was Mentioned in Dispatches once again. Savige now returned home. Speculation was that at the age of fifty-one he would retire, but Japan's entry into the war changed that idea.

Far from retiring, Savige was promoted to Major-General and given command of the 3rd Division. This was a huge promotion and a huge responsibility. In the New Guinea campaign, the Division fought in the tough Wau/Salamaua region. It was hand to hand warfare. Savige's role was not to implement and execute tactical operations so much as to provide properly for his men and care for their individual safety and morale. This is where Savige excelled. He was often in the front line and made a point of always wearing his red-banded Major-General's cap to show that he was not hiding from the enemy in anonymity. Gavin Keating, in his article on Savige in the *Australian Dictionary of Biography*, writes:

His direction of the campaign was characterised by his encouragement of subordinate commanders, by his concern for his men, and by the way his divisional headquarters provided particularly effective artillery support.

On the point of occupying Salamaua the 17th Brigade was relieved. The campaign remains a feather in Savige's cap. His reward was to be appointed Companion of the Order of the Bath (CB), one of the most ancient of British orders of chivalry.

The last stage of Savige's active military career came with his appointment as Lieutenant-General and Commander of I Corps (later named II Corps), with a total of 30,000 men under his command. His appointment was again criticised by the 'professional soldier' elements in the army. At the heart of this sentiment was that Savige was always on close terms with Sir Thomas Blamey, overall commander of the Australian army, and another citizen-soldier. It was thought, without evidence, that Blamey had favoured Savige throughout the war beyond his abilities. However, subsequent analysis has always vindicated Savige's actions when in command. In his new role, Savige commanded II Corps in the Bougainville campaign. The Solomon Islands, which include Bougainville, had been an Australian mandate before the war. The Australian troops fought in the understanding they were taking back their own territory. The Americans on Bougainville handed over operations to the Australian forces and went on to pursue their liberation of the Philippines. In that sense, the Bougainville campaign was a 'mopping-up' operation. By the time the war ended in August, 1945, some 520 Australian troops had lost their lives, while 1500 had been wounded. In early September the operation concluded. The commander of Japanese forces on Bougainville surrendered to Lieutenant-General Stanley Savige. Photos held in the Australian War Museum show a grim-faced, bespectacled Savige accepting the Japanese surrender at Torokina.

Stanley Savige's work for the nation was not yet complete, however. He was the National Coordinator of Demobilisation and Dispersal for eight months until May, 1946. This was a huge task as there were 600,000 service personnel to be placed back into civilian life. He then resumed his business career, serving on the Boards of the Olympic Tyre Company, Moran & Cato, and the State Savings Bank, as well as chairing the War Gratuity Board. He led Anzac Day marches in Melbourne, and remained active in several ex-service organisations. In 1950 he was elevated to Knight Commander of the British Empire (KBE). In 1953 he and Lady Lilian represented Legacy at the coronation of Queen Elizabeth II.

Lady Savige died in March, 1954, and Sir Stanley survived for just two more months, the cause of his death being coronary artery disease. 'He was just worn out,' one of his family said. He was given a funeral with full military honours at St Paul's Cathedral in Melbourne. In his address, Bishop John McKie commented, 'Sir Stanley's greatest virtue was humanity. He had great consideration for his troops. He thought that they were not there just to be used, but to be helped.' A crowd of 3,000 mourners attended his burial at Kew Cemetery (now Boroondara).

Savige's name continues to be honoured. In August, 2006, a bronze portrait bust on a fine granite pedestal commemorating Sir Stanley was unveiled in Legacy Place in Morwell. Legacy Place is an urban art project devoted to the memory of Sir Stanley Savige and is a stone's throw away from his birthplace in Tarwin Street. The inscription on the memorial says:

This Memorial was erected by the Citizens of Morwell to honour a Great Humanitarian and Great Australian.

At the time of Savige's death, John Hetherington, a leading journalist and war correspondent, wrote a memorial tribute to Sir Stanley Savige. He headed his piece, 'A Man's Man'. Savige was, above all, a man who understood men, he wrote. He went on:

Savige did not pretend to be a military genius, but only a commander who knew his way round the battlefield because he had learned his soldiering the hard way.... He had no trace of vanity, but he did pride himself on his ability to handle men or blokes, to use his own term. "You can never really know blokes unless you have worked alongside them," he once told me. "I reckon the best education I ever had was swinging a pick as one of a gang of navvies when I was a young fellow."

Hetherington ended with a warm tribute to the closeness between Savige and his Commander and friend, Sir Thomas Blamey:

Savige esteemed and admired Blamey above all men. His most cherished possession was a personal letter which Blamey wrote him soon after the war ended. "Your services during the period of the war years," Blamey wrote, "present a remarkable record. It is, too, a record of achievement and of success which has been marked by great hardship, and on many occasions, as I know well, you have had to follow a lonely road. This you have done calmly and quietly, and on every occasion the event has proved you right".

One can hardly pay sufficient honour to this remarkable man, Lieutenant-General Sir Stanley George Savige, KBE, CB, DSO, MC, ED, a man of character and compassion who has few equals in courage, skill and achievement and whose record is second to none in service to the Australian nation.

DAVID WILLIAMSON

... who went to school in Bairnsdale and became the most-produced playwright in Australia's history.

David Williamson writes of his years in Bairnsdale with obvious affection. He arrived in 1954 when he was twelve just in time to start at Bairnsdale High School in Form 1. David's father had been transferred to the Bairnsdale branch of the State Savings Bank, and David moved with his parents and younger brother into the Bank house in Pearson Street, close to the middle of town.

In his memoir, *Home Truths*, Williamson describes his introduction to his new school with this comic reminiscence:

We have all seen the Westerns where the new guy in town belts open the batwing doors and strides into the saloon, hands hovering over his six-gun, and challenges the fastest gun-slinger in town. Having been the wrestling champion of my city school, mostly because my enormous height gave me great leverage, I thrust the doors aside and demanded to know the name of their best wrestler. They turned and pointed to Foster Cornelius Bibron ... Foster took one look and approximately ten seconds to have me pinned flat on my back.

Luckily he was a lovely guy who spared me too much pain, and we became instant friends.

David was a bright student and earned the nickname, 'Genius'. However, in typical schoolboy fashion, he dumbed himself down so as to stick with the crowd. He writes amusingly of the schoolroom pranks and entanglements with both girl and boy friends. Helen Kennedy, Judy Morecroft, Margaret McAllister, Bob Rankin, Dick Cugley, and Norm Seaton are mentioned in the text, and he gives the impression that he became 'one of the boys' despite his extreme self-consciousness because of his height. Some Bairnsdale High students of that era still meet regularly, Williamson included, and the school's blog site indicates how strong feeling is for the old school.

The school's Principal at that time was WD (Bill) Gibbs, who is remembered as a wise and compassionate man. Williamson's great joy, however, was to have an inspiring English teacher, Alan ('Boof') McLeod:

Alan had the charisma and gravitas of Spencer Tracy. When Boof walked into the class and looked at us one by one with his x-ray eyes, there was instant and total silence. ... Boof brought the [Shakespearean] *texts to life with booming conviction and authority, acting out the roles, unearthing the motives, exploring the characters and showing us that the emotional needs for respect, acceptance, love, revenge, status and power four hundred years ago in a land far away still drove us.*

One can understand how the understanding of human nature learnt there in that faraway place and time stood Williamson in good stead in later years as he explored the depths of human complexity in his plays.

Alongside his growing love for the English language, Williamson was also gifted on the mathematical side. In the 'fifties it was almost automatic that boys who showed all-round ability would be directed towards Maths/Science subjects rather than the humanities. So it was for Williamson. Perhaps because of this his senior years at the school saw no let-up in his predilection for amusement and misbehaviour, so much so that the Principal advised his father to place him in another school if he was to succeed academically. Hence, Williamson was packed off to Melbourne to board with his grandmother while he completed his Sixth Form at University High School. He actually repeated the year after his moderate results at his first attempt.

Williamson was by now a confirmed left-winger in politics, a modest musician who played the wrong sort of music for his trendy times, and, with his father, an enthusiastic Collingwood supporter. As well, he resonated deeply with good literature, Hemingway and Eliot in particular. Despite all this he chose to do Mechanical Engineering at Melbourne University. He was to become, in his own words, a 'misfit engineer'. His real education came from his partying with his gregarious and colourful friends, many of whom were to be later transmuted into characters in his plays. His reading of modern authors continued, leaving him with *'the question that still obsessed me ... why was there so much savage conflict between people, between political systems, between nations?'* He was to work at that problem over the next fifty years – over the whole course of his writing.

Williamson looked back very happily on his Gippsland days, and when one of his old friends from Bairnsdale High, Norm Seaton, rang him to ask if he would like to spend his first Christmas vacation from university working with him at Wilsons Promontory he quickly accepted. The job was clearing campsites and the man in charge was the famed Olympic runner, John Landy. Williamson was very impressed with Landy. Later he wrote a mini-series for the BBC on the Bannister-Landy duel for the sub-four-minute mile. Another of the student-workers at the Prom at the time was Carol Cranby. Later she was to become David's first wife.

Williamson's second Christmas vacation was spent 'getting experience' at the Mount Lyell copper mine near Queenstown on the inhospitable west coast of Tasmania. It was a hard time. He learnt more about the destruction of the environment than about engineering, although his observation of the diverse company of miners provided fruitful material for his emerging writer's mind.

In his third year, Williamson was most distinguished for his part in writing and acting for the annual Engineers' revue. The sound of the audience's laughter 'planted a strong impression of the excitement of theatre and the feedback it offered'. However, he was completely out of his depth with his engineering course and sat for only two of his exams. One of them asked for a discussion of the merits of SAP. Williamson had no idea what SAP stood for (actually, sintered aluminium products) and wrote a long essay on South Australian Peanuts! It was the end of his Melbourne University career, but a sympathetic professor arranged for him to be accepted into Engineering at the new Monash University. Settling down (and maybe because he was more distant from his previous fun-loving companions) he did well enough to graduate two years later. Williamson sums up his position at this point:

I was now qualified to practise in a profession concerned with all things mechanical but still unable to diagnose or repair even the simplest problem under the bonnet of my car.

Nevertheless, Williamson continued with Engineering. He got a job with General Motors where he designed a hand-brake, which, he said, 'if ever installed, parked Holdens would shrug off my feeble restraint and career down hills, and the resulting lawsuits would bankrupt the firm'. His employment at GMH didn't last much longer! Williamson's interests lay elsewhere. His social conscience threw him inevitably into opposition to the Vietnam War which occurred at this time. His outspokenness led to his election as President of the Melbourne Youth Campaign against Conscription.

Needing employment and without other professional skills, he applied for a job as a lecturer in the diploma course in Mechanical Engineering being offered at Swinburne College of Technology.

That was late in 1965 and before he took up his appointment in the New Year he and Carol were married, on 3 December in that year. I wonder if David was aware that he married on the anniversary of the Eureka Stockade! The marriage was not to last.

Despite his success in scripting amateur theatricals, Williamson was stuck on being a novelist. He put together his first attempt. Carol was not encouraging in her reaction, and neither were his friends who 'ran when they saw me coming'. 'What I thought were black comic masterpieces were in fact very poor and overwrought imitations of Joseph Heller'. He sent his novel to the tip.

At this point, Williamson once again ran into his old friend from Bairnsdale, Bob Rankin, who was now doing Psychology at Melbourne University. David decided that through a study of psychology he might come to some answers concerning his eternal quest to discover the springs of the 'omnipresent human capacity for conflict'. Consequently, he enrolled in an MA (Prelim) in Psychology at Melbourne. He found the course something of a disappointment. However, it was at this time that Williamson had the road-to Damascus moment that converted him from frustrated novelist to nascent playwright.

During a production of Arthur Miller's *Incident at Vichy* at the Russell Street Theatre, he explains:

I did have a strong and sudden conviction that writing plays was what I could do and was meant to do. I loved the intense connection between the actors onstage and the living, breathing audience absorbing every word.

Williamson went home and 'dashed off' his first play, a short piece, *You've got to get on, Jack*, which was grounded in his experience of the bullying and intimidation he had seen amongst the ragged company of workers during his time at Queenstown, now some years in the past. The script, however, languished for some time before eventually coming to the surface.

Meanwhile, Williamson, now madly enthused, 'dashed off' several more plays. One of them, *The Indecent Exposure of Anthony East*, was, this time, a full-length production. The play, heavily influenced by the American writer, JP Donleavy, was put on by the Tin Alley Players, the student drama group at Melbourne University, in 1968 and ran for three nights. Williamson constantly championed the need to have a genuinely Australian theatre, and although he was far from enthusiastic about his *Anthony East*, he applauded the fact that an Australian playwright had been brought to the stage. He wrote in the programme notes for the production:

There is a belief that an Australian writer is an inferior creature. This belief may not be shaken by tonight's performance – but nevertheless I should like to thank the producer for helping to get this play into a shape which is at least workable, and for his courage in taking an 'Australian' production. We need an Australian Theatre because we are not Americans, Britons or Swedes, and, until local producers are prepared to do the hard work of finding potential playwrights, helping them to raise rough drafts and enabling them to learn from their own mistakes, we won't get it.

In 1970, his first-born play, *You've got to get on, Jack*, was accepted by Betty Burstall's La Mama theatre in Carlton. This was the real thing. No amateur group of university students this time, but a leading company of professionals. Williamson was ecstatic. He pokes fun at himself: 'Vivid waking dreams of standing ovations and cries of 'Author, Author!' blotted out the world around me'. The reality was rather different. Williamson describes what happened:

Carol and I and a few friends were in the audience when Finney, Spence and Phelan, these three giants of the Carlton scene, whom I hadn't even met, walked on to the tiny stage of the sixty-seat theatre with my script in their hands. Nervous but hugely excited, I waited. The actors didn't know I was in the audience as I hadn't even told Betty that I was coming. ... Finney held up the script and said that they'd got this script from a guy called Williamson. It wasn't very good, but they'd pick out a few lines to show how good acting could bring a dead script to life. They then started on the line, 'Who asked you shithead?', doing it many different ways to display their virtuosity. The audience roared with laughter. Instead of triumph, this was total humiliation. I slunk out afterwards without meeting the actors. This was the end of all my delusions that I could become a writer of any kind.

Far from it being the end, Williamson was in fact just beginning. The play was put on in its entirety a little later, after Burstall realised that it did indeed have merit. And within two years three of Williamson's plays had been given major productions. These included some of his best work – *The Coming of Stork*, *Don's Party*, and *The Removalists*.

The Coming of Stork (1971) is largely autobiographical. Stork is a hugely tall character like Williamson. He's sacked from his job (at General Motors!) and moves in with some friends, as Williamson had done. The action and much of the dialogue comes directly from Williamson's earlier bachelor days. Some of his friends in this and in later plays were not happy to see themselves portrayed warts and all on stage – and some, later, on screen. The play was made into a film some ten years later, under the title, *Stork*, and included well-known actors Bruce Spence, Jacki Weaver, Graeme Blundell, Terry Norris, and Max Gillies. It has been labelled 'one of the first ocker comedies'.

The next year came *The Removalists*, a major success, and later made into a film. It won an AWGIE Award and, when taken to London, saw Williamson nominated as 'most promising playwright' by the London Evening Standard. The impact of this new force-majeure of Australian theatre is well-illustrated by this account of the play's discovery by the leading director, John Bell, then at the Nimrod Theatre in Sydney:

We were all pretty busy and not well organised when it came to play reading. Some scripts languished for months, or got lost, and we were frequently bawled out by frustrated or disappointed playwrights. Anna [Anna Volska, his actor wife] *helped me sort through the pile of scripts and one night yelled out, "Wow! Now here's a play!" – or words to that effect. It was called The Removalists by a Melbourne writer, David Williamson. I concurred with Anna's judgement and read the play in one sitting. In fact I couldn't put it down. Here was an authentic Australian voice with a wry, mordant – and hilarious – sense of theatre. David's ear for colloquial idiom was uncanny and this explains the scale of his initial success, which he followed through with in Don's Party, A Handful of Friends, The Club and others. Australian audiences were thrilled with the authenticity of his mimicry as well as the gallery of his most successful characters, all variants of the likeable arch-bastard along the lines of Barry Humphries' Les Patterson.*

Don's Party, which quickly followed, is probably Williamson's best known work. It also was made into a film. The Wikipedia summary of the plot is as follows. From it we can grasp the kind of social-interaction comedy-drama material Williamson works with in many of his plays:

Don Henderson is a schoolteacher living with his wife Kath and baby son in the Melbourne suburb of Lower Plenty. On the night of the 1969 federal election Don invites a small group of friends to celebrate a predicted ALP election victory, much to the dismay of his wife. To the party come Mal, Don's university mentor, and his bitter wife Jenny, sex-obsessed Cooley and his latest girlfriend, nineteen-year-old Susan, Evan, a dentist, and his beautiful artist wife Kerry. Somehow, two Liberal supporters, Simon and Jody also come.

As the party wears on it becomes clear that the Labor party, which is supported by Don and most of the guests, is not winning. As a result, alcohol consumption increases, and the sniping between Don and his male friends about their failed aspirations gets uglier, as does their behaviour toward the women. Mack, a design engineer whose wife has just left him, pulls out a nude photo of her for his friends' approval. Crass womaniser Cooley pursues the available women. The disillusioned wives exchange tales of their husbands' sub-par sexual performance. By the end of the night, Don and some of his friends have begun to grasp the emptiness of their compromised lives.

A later film version is set in Sydney and is more explicit in nature. Some were shocked by what they saw as the coarseness of the text. In defence, Williamson says, "I didn't enjoy being an enfant terrible. I just wanted to say, 'Look, this is the Australia I know and have come to understand'".

A huge volume of work then flowed from Williamson's pen – a total of fifty-five plays and twenty-four film scripts that he wrote sometimes alone and sometimes with others. The subject matter of his work broadened to include topical subjects such as the screenplay for the film, *Balibo*, which dealt with the killing of five journalists during the Indonesian invasion of East Timor in 1975. Another example is the writing of the screenplay for the acclaimed film, *Gallipoli*. Sandra Bates, writing a Foreword to the Currency Press's 2012 *Collected Plays*, describes his complete works as …

a remarkable body of work which, if read from the beginning (or better still seen) gives great insight into what has happened in Australia over these four decades: a social history at least as accurate and certainly much more entertaining than a treatise or dry history book covering those forty years.

Meanwhile, Williamson's private life moved on. The marriage with Carol eventually failed and in 1974 David married Kristin Green who had worked with him on the set of *The Removalists*. Two of Williamson's five children – Felix and Rory - have worked in theatre. In 2001, in a revival of *The Coming* of *Stork*, Rory had the title role, while the play was produced by Felix's theatre company. The marriage with Kristin has continued to the present day, despite several difficulties and estrangements. They now have homes in Sydney and near Noosa.

In his memoir, *Home Truths*, Williamson shows himself to be very sensitive to criticism. He kept a book of press notices about his work. When challenged he hit back hard. When, for instance, some criticised his *Money and Friends* (1991) he defended himself fiercely. Williamson acknowledged that he was somewhat thin-skinned regarding criticism. As in all things, Williamson was brutally honest with himself and his misdemeanours and peccadilloes. But he would have laughed, I should think, at the review of one of his plays, *Heretic*, by the comic team, The Chasers. Under the heading, 'Cast trapped in hull of David Williamson's play', the report read:

Hopes are fading for the cast of David Williamson's play Heretic, trapped six days ago when a flimsy premise collapsed, sending a number of overbearing symbols crashing to the ground, cutting the characters off from the rest of the world. The play mounts a veiled and ultimately unsuccessful attack on feminism, and the sexual revolution generally, by attacking the anthropologist Margaret Mead. The cast immediately went backstage and improvised in an attempt to right the wounded script. ... For some days after the tragedy a feeble scratching sound could be heard coming from the vicinity of the play. This has now been identified as dialogue.

The Chasers' view has not been shared by many over the course of Williamson's vast output. On the contrary, he has been awarded an Order of Australia (AO), the Australian Writers Guild Awgie Award for best stage play and best script (for *The Removalists*), and honorary doctorates of several universities, including Monash, Sydney, Queensland and Swinburne. For the Australian Film Institute, he has won the best screenplay award on four occasions – for *Don's Party*, *Gallipoli*, *Travelling North*, and *Balibo*. In 2005, Williamson received the JC Williamson award from Live Performance Australia (LPA), their highest honour, for his life's work in live performance. Williamson is one of sixty Australians who have been honoured in the Sydney Writers Walk at Circular Quay in Sydney. Each plaque contains a sentence or two from their work. For Williamson, the quotation given, from his play, Emerald City, are these satirical words:

In Melbourne, all views are equally depressing, so there's no point in having one. ... No one in Sydney ever wastes time debating the meaning of life – it's getting yourself a water frontage. People devote a lifetime to the quest.

It is always difficult for a writer to type the last full stop. In 2023, just as this book was going to press, it was announced that Williamson had come out of retirement to write a new play, *The Great Divide*, which will be staged in Sydney in March, 2024. It deals with what Williamson sees as the growing inequalities in Australian society. Williamson's decision to take up the gauntlet once more is a reminder that society is never static and that we will always have need of social critics to puncture the hypocrisies and duplicities that arise in any community.

We might leave the last word in honour of David Williamson with Sandra Bates:

So what is it that makes David's success unique in Australia's theatre history? I believe it has a lot to do with his ability to see and understand Australia's current circumstances, our society's circumstances right here and now. ... Is there a thread that connects his vast body of work?... I would say that at the basis of almost all his work the need for tolerance in our society is that connecting thread, and is probably why his work is so popular. Many of his characters are deeply flawed, but at the core of his work there is a desire for a better society, a more tolerant society, and even these deeply flawed characters mostly struggle to lead a better life, a more tolerant life.

Perhaps David Williamson never found his way to understanding the roots of human conflict. Who could?! On the other hand he might have found the way to deal with it – through tolerance for one another. Perhaps that –the need for tolerance - was the most important lesson David Williamson was learning during those years of his growing-up at Bairnsdale High School!

www.ingramcontent.com/pod-product-compliance
Lightning Source LLC
Chambersburg PA
CBHW020322010526
44107CB00054B/1940